The
PEANUT BUTTER
Cookbook

Mable Hoffman

Illustrations by
Michelle Burchard

HPBooks

HPBooks
Published by The Berkley Publishing Group
200 Madison Avenue
New York, NY 10016

Copyright © 1996 by Mable Hoffman
Book design by Irving Perkins Associates
Cover photograph by George Kerrigan
Interior illustrations by Michelle Burchard

First edition: July 1996

Published simultaneously in Canada.

The Putnam Berkley World Wide Web site address is
http://www.berkley.com

Library of Congress Cataloging-in-Publication Data

Hoffman, Mable.
    The peanut butter cookbook / Mable Hoffman. — 1st ed.
        p. cm.
    ISBN 1-55788-243-6
    1. Cookery (Peanut butter) 2. Peanut butter. I. Title.
TX814.5.P38H64   1996
641.6′56596—dc20   95-51740
                                                           CIP
        Printed in the United States of America

        10   9   8   7   6   5   4   3   2   1

NOTICE: The information printed in this book is true and
complete to the best of our knowledge. All recommendations
are made without any guarantees on the part of the author or
the publisher. The author and publisher disclaim all liability in
connection with the use of this information.

Acknowledgments

Special thanks to Jan Robertson for her overall assistance and recipe testing for this book. Her input reflects trends and eating habits of young families throughout the country.

Also, I am very grateful to Mike Robertson for his long hours and frustrating computer processing.

Last but not least, this project would not be possible without the cooperation and advice of Jeanette Egan.

Contents

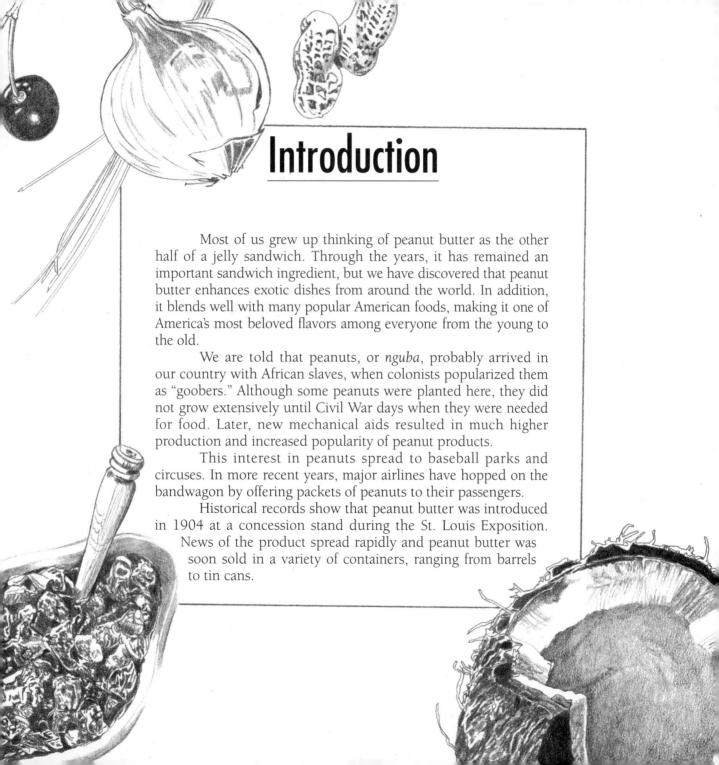

Introduction

Most of us grew up thinking of peanut butter as the other half of a jelly sandwich. Through the years, it has remained an important sandwich ingredient, but we have discovered that peanut butter enhances exotic dishes from around the world. In addition, it blends well with many popular American foods, making it one of America's most beloved flavors among everyone from the young to the old.

We are told that peanuts, or *nguba*, probably arrived in our country with African slaves, when colonists popularized them as "goobers." Although some peanuts were planted here, they did not grow extensively until Civil War days when they were needed for food. Later, new mechanical aids resulted in much higher production and increased popularity of peanut products.

This interest in peanuts spread to baseball parks and circuses. In more recent years, major airlines have hopped on the bandwagon by offering packets of peanuts to their passengers.

Historical records show that peanut butter was introduced in 1904 at a concession stand during the St. Louis Exposition. News of the product spread rapidly and peanut butter was soon sold in a variety of containers, ranging from barrels to tin cans.

When the demand for peanut butter increased during World War I, manufacturers switched to glass jars. Within a few years the gritty peanut butters were churned like butter, resulting in a smoother product. Also, a shelf-stable product that did not require refrigeration was introduced. Later a chunky-style peanut butter was created by adding chopped peanuts at the end of the manufacturing process.

By the 1940s, peanut butter had become an all-American favorite and has continued to be one of our staple foods. Today, peanut butter is so popular with adults that it has its own fan club of more than 60,000 people from all 50 states. According to a survey made by the fan club, the average 18-ounce jar of peanut butter lasts from 2 weeks to a month.

Peanut Butter Production

After peanuts are harvested, they are inspected, shelled and delivered to peanut butter manufacturers. At that time they are roasted and blanched to remove the thin skins around each nut. Then the peanuts are heated to about 170 degrees Fahrenheit and ground until smooth. Just before being pumped into jars, the product has all air bubbles removed to ensure a smooth texture.

Major Kinds of Peanut Butter

Regular

This type is available in smooth or crunchy. Sugars and hydrogenated vegetable oils are added.

All Natural

Old-fashioned peanut butter is available in smooth and crunchy. No preservatives or stabilizers are added. It should be stirred and stored in the refrigerator before using.

Reduced-Fat

It has 25 percent less fat than regular peanut butter but the same number of calories. Soy protein is added to replace part of the peanuts. It is available in smooth and crunchy.

Low-Sodium and Reduced-Sugar

This type contains 2 grams of sugars (sugar plus molasses) per serving as compared to double that amount for regular peanut butter.

Roasted Honey Nut

Sweetened with honey and high fructose corn syrup, plus molasses.

Smooth or Crunchy

Ask peanut butter fans whether they prefer the smooth or crunchy style, and you will get very strong opinions on each side.

Our recipes were tested with regular smooth peanut butter unless crunchy is indicated in the ingredients list. If you have a definite preference for either kind, you can substitute your favorite.

When substituting crunchy peanut butter for a recipe calling for the smooth variety, the result will have slightly less body and peanut butter flavor. On the other hand, when you substitute smooth for crunchy peanut butter, the result will have slightly more body and a creamier texture, resulting in a fuller peanut butter flavor.

Baking with reduced-fat peanut butter will result in a slightly drier product.

Peanut Butter Nutrients

Although the word *butter* is on the label and the texture is quite *buttery*, peanut butter has no cholesterol or animal fat. Actually, it is a member of the pea family. Peanuts are high in niacin, zinc, protein and fiber.

Storing Peanut Butter

Keep it in a cool, dry place. At intervals, check the expiration date on the jar.

Tips for Using Peanut Butter

- If you don't think you will use the peanut butter before the expiration date on the jar, keep it in the refrigerator to extend the fresh peanut flavor.
- Peanut butter is difficult to remove from utensils and bowls if left standing. Either pre-rinse or soak dishes ahead of time to make them easier to clean.
- If you store peanut butter in the refrigerator, remove it about 30 minutes before trying to spread it on a sandwich or use it in a recipe.

Snacks & Appetizers

Snacking is a favorite pastime for people of all ages, from toddlers to seniors, and peanut butter is one of the most popular ingredients associated with this practice. At a very young age, many of us started with peanut butter and crackers, then we graduated to more sophisticated combinations.

After-school snacks play an important role in the lives of most children. They like to refuel with food that will keep away hunger pains until dinner. That's when we offer them Fruit Leather Roll-Ups or a Banana Orange Yogurt Shake.

Grown-ups are avid snackers, too. In addition, they enjoy appetizers made with combinations of peanut butter in more adult favorites such as Occidental Endive Appetizer or Shrimp & Snow Peas with Party Dip.

Breadstick Turkey Roll-Ups

Pick up a package of thinly sliced meat at the deli or supermarket.

1/4 cup peanut butter
12 very thin slices smoked turkey or beef
6 long thin breadsticks (about 9 1/2 inches long)

Spread thin layer of peanut butter on one side of sliced turkey. Break each breadstick in half. Place breadstick half on one end of each slice of turkey. Roll up. Makes 12 roll-ups.

Peanut butter is easier to spread if it is at room temperature.

Popcorn Snacks

Old-fashioned popcorn combines with peanut butter and seasonings for a pick-me-up snack.

1/2 cup peanut butter
1/4 cup brown sugar, lightly packed
1/2 cup honey
2 tablespoons vegetable oil
1 teaspoon vanilla extract

1 (3 1/2-oz.) can flaked coconut
1/2 cup chopped dried peaches or apricots
1/4 cup sesame seeds, toasted
1 cup quick uncooked rolled oats
3 cups popped popcorn

Preheat oven to 300°F (150°C). In a medium saucepan, combine peanut butter, brown sugar, honey and oil over medium heat and stir until well blended. Stir in vanilla, coconut, peaches or apricots, sesame seeds, oats and popcorn. Spread mixture in a 15 x 10-inch jelly-roll pan. Bake in preheated oven 25 to 35 minutes, stirring twice. Cool. Store leftovers in an airtight container. Makes about 5 cups.

Banana Orange Yogurt Shake

Just combine everything together in a blender and it's ready in a jiffy.

8 oz. (1 cup) tropical or apricot-pineapple–flavored low-fat yogurt
3 tablespoons peanut butter
1/4 cup nonfat dry milk powder
1 large ripe banana, peeled and cut into chunks
3/4 cup orange juice
2 tablespoons honey
Ground nutmeg

In a blender, combine yogurt, peanut butter, dry milk powder, banana, orange juice and honey. Blend until smooth. Sprinkle with nutmeg. Makes 2 cups.

Bacon & Apple–Topped Bagels

A healthy and hearty breakfast or after-school snack.

2 bagels
1/4 cup peanut butter
2 tablespoons unsweetened applesauce
2 slices bacon, cooked crisp, drained and crumbled
1 tablespoon plain yogurt
1 apple, cored and cut into 20 thin slices

Split bagels in half crosswise. In a medium bowl, combine peanut butter and applesauce. Stir in bacon and yogurt. Spread on cut sides of bagels. Top each with apple slices. Serve immediately. Makes 4 halves.

Sweet 'n' Spicy Spread

An appetizing fuss-free snack that can be put together at a moment's notice.

1/4 cup crunchy peanut butter
1/2 cup apricot jam
1 tablespoon finely chopped canned green chiles, drained
1 teaspoon sweet hot mustard
1 (3-oz.) package cream cheese, softened
Assorted crackers

In a small bowl, combine peanut butter, jam, chiles and mustard. Place cream cheese on a medium plate. Top with peanut butter mixture. Spread a bit of cream cheese and peanut butter mixture over each cracker. Makes enough for 30 to 35 crackers.

Stuffed Apricot Halves

The coconut and pineapple add tropical flavors to the peanut butter.

1/2 cup crunchy peanut butter
1/4 cup shredded coconut
1 (8-oz.) can crushed pineapple, well drained (see Note)
2 teaspoons finely chopped candied ginger
About 60 dried apricot halves or pitted prunes

In a small bowl, combine peanut butter, coconut, pineapple and ginger. Spoon about 1 teaspoon into center of each half apricot or prune. Makes about 60.

It is important that the pineapple be well drained. Pour into a strainer and press with the back of a spoon to remove liquid. The liquid can be used for cooking or added to a juice drink.

Peanut Butter & Jelly Tortilla Roll-Ups

Tuck several roll-ups into a small plastic bag, then into your backpack to enjoy during a hike.

4 (6-inch) flour tortillas
1/4 cup peanut butter
1/4 cup grape jelly or strawberry preserves

Spread each flour tortilla with about 1 tablespoon peanut butter and 1 tablespoon jelly. Carefully roll up. Wrap in foil or plastic wrap and keep in the refrigerator for a snack or quick lunch. Makes 4 roll-ups.

Gingered Peanut Carrot Spread

A quick and healthful pickup for breakfast or snack time.

2 carrots, peeled and grated
1/3 cup raisins, chopped
1/2 cup crunchy peanut butter
1/4 cup mayonnaise
1/2 teaspoon ground ginger
3 hamburger buns or English muffins, halved
Chopped peanuts

In a medium bowl, combine carrots, raisins, peanut butter, mayonnaise and ginger. Spread on cut sides of each bun. Top with chopped peanuts. Makes 6 open-face sandwiches.

Fruit Leather Roll-Ups

Children enjoy this nutritious snack.

2 grape or strawberry fruit leather roll-ups
2 tablespoons peanut butter
1 pear or apple

Unroll fruit leather. Spread about 1 tablespoon peanut butter on one side of each. Cut each into 8 wedges. Peel, core and slice pear or apple into 16 very thin wedges. Place slice of pear or apple on each wedge; roll up. Makes 16 roll-ups.

Variation

Substitute banana strips for the pear or apple.

Peanut Butter & Bacon Pâté

Be sure to finely chop the fruit in the chutney before adding it to the remaining ingredients.

2 tablespoons margarine or butter
4 fresh mushrooms, finely chopped
2 green onions, finely chopped
1/2 cup crunchy peanut butter
1 (3-oz.) package cream cheese, softened
2 tablespoons fruit chutney, finely chopped
2 slices bacon, cooked crisp, drained and crumbled
1 tablespoon sesame seeds, toasted
Crackers

In a small pan, melt margarine over medium heat. Add mushrooms and onions. Cook, stirring occasionally, about 5 minutes or until softened. Remove from heat. Stir in peanut butter, cream cheese, chutney and bacon. Spoon into a small bowl. Sprinkle with sesame seeds. Cover and refrigerate 2 to 3 hours or until firm. Serve on crackers. Makes about 1 cup.

Occidental Endive Appetizer

Crisp leaves of Belgian endive make an impressive "holder" for appetizer fillings.

2 boneless, skinless chicken breast halves
1 tablespoon vegetable oil (optional)
1/4 cup teriyaki sauce
2 teaspoons honey
2 tablespoons peanut butter
1/8 teaspoon red pepper flakes
About 2 heads Belgian endive

Cook chicken in hot oil over medium heat until white in center or gently simmer in a little water until done (about 10 minutes). Let cool. Chop chicken coarsely, then process in a food processor or grinder until finely ground. Combine with teriyaki sauce, honey, peanut butter and pepper flakes. Pull apart individual endive leaves. Spoon filling into center of each leaf. Makes 20 to 22 filled leaves.

Variation

Substitute 2 cups chopped cooked chicken or turkey for the chicken breast.

Shrimp & Snow Peas with Party Dip

This impressive shrimp appetizer comes with an unusual dip.

2 1/2 to 3 oz. snow peas (about 30)
1 lb. cooked shelled medium shrimp (about 30)
1 tablespoon freshly squeezed lemon juice
1/4 cup peanut butter
1 clove garlic, peeled
3 tablespoons mango chutney (fruit and syrup)
1 teaspoon grated gingerroot
4 teaspoons soy sauce
1/8 teaspoon red pepper flakes

Trim ends off pea pods. Drop snow peas into a saucepan of boiling water and boil 1 to 2 minutes or until flexible. Rinse in cold water; drain. Wrap a cooked snow pea around each cooked shrimp; secure with a wooden pick.

In a blender or food processor, combine lemon juice, peanut butter, garlic, chutney, gingerroot, soy sauce and pepper flakes; process until blended. Pour sauce into a small bowl. To eat, dip each snow pea–covered shrimp into chutney mixture. Makes about 30 appetizers.

Peanut Butter & Bacon Squares

A surprise combination of ethnic flavors results in a favorite appetizer.

2 tablespoons plum jam
1/2 cup peanut butter
2 teaspoons soy sauce
2 tablespoons mayonnaise
2 tablespoons finely chopped green onion
6 slices bread
4 or 5 slices bacon, cooked crisp, drained and coarsely crumbled

Combine jam with peanut butter, soy sauce, mayonnaise and green onion in a small bowl. Remove crusts from bread; lightly toast. Spread about 2 tablespoons mixture on each slice of toast and sprinkle with bacon. Place slices in a broiler pan; broil until topping is bubbly. Cut each slice into quarters. Serve warm. Makes 24 appetizers.

Carrot Peanut Pâté

It will be soft when warm, but just the right texture after chilling.

3 green onions, sliced (about 1/4 cup)
3 medium carrots, peeled and thinly sliced
1 clove garlic, crushed
1/2 teaspoon curry powder
1/2 cup chicken broth or bouillon
1/3 cup crunchy peanut butter
2 tablespoons margarine or butter
Sliced uncooked zucchini or cauliflower and/or crackers

In a 2-quart saucepan, combine onions, carrots, garlic, curry powder and broth. Bring to a boil, reduce heat and simmer, covered, 8 to 10 minutes or until carrots are tender. Process carrot mixture in a blender or food processor until pureed. Blend in peanut butter and margarine or butter. Spoon into a serving bowl. Cover and refrigerate 2 or 3 hours. Serve as a spread for vegetables and/or crackers. Makes 1 2/3 cups.

Mandarin Ham Roll-Ups

Substitute seedless fresh tangerines for mandarin oranges whenever they are available.

6 thin slices cooked ham
3 tablespoons crunchy peanut butter
18 canned mandarin orange segments, drained
1 tablespoon sweet hot mustard
1 tablespoon orange marmalade
1/4 cup teriyaki sauce

Cut each slice of ham into 3 strips about 1 1/3 x 4 inches. Spread about 1/2 teaspoon peanut butter over one side of each. Top each with 1 section of mandarin orange; roll up. Secure each roll-up with a wooden pick.

In a small bowl, combine mustard, marmalade and teriyaki sauce. To eat, dip roll-ups into sauce. Makes 18 roll-ups.

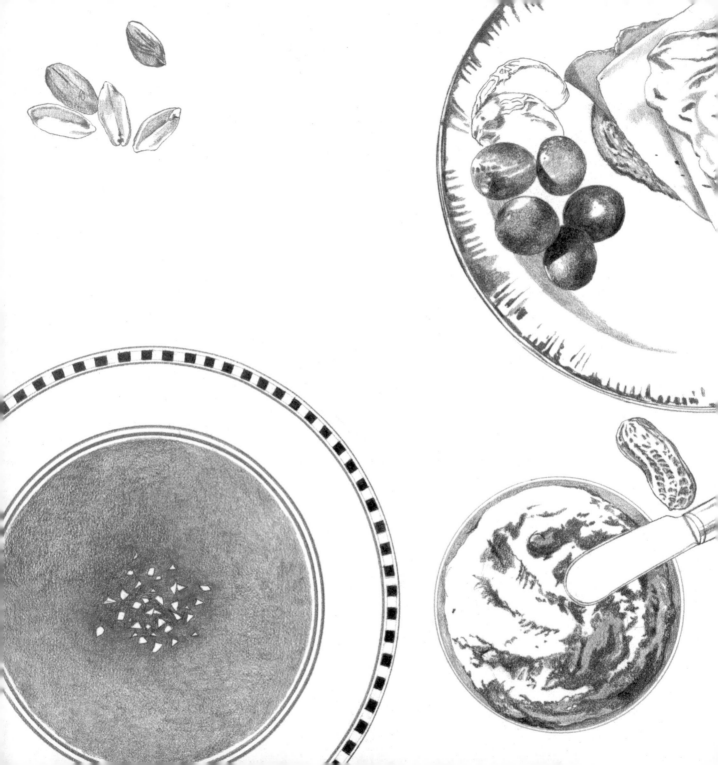

Sandwiches & Soups

Sandwiches are served for almost all occasions and any time of day, from breakfast to midnight. Ingredients range from the ever-popular traditional meat and cheese combinations to the more time-consuming miniature party shapes. Peanut butter and jelly might not be considered sophisticated, but it is a favorite with thousands of people of all ages.

For special occasions, I like to find an unusual variety of bread at the bakery or supermarket, spread it with a compatible filling, then tuck in a few leaves of lettuce.

Don't overlook the combination of sandwiches with soup for a casual meal while you and your family are watching a favorite ball game or theatrical production on television. Our Peanut Butter Soup is the most requested soup in my family.

Open-Face Pesto Prosciutto Sandwiches

A colorful unique open-face sandwich with fresh herb accents.

1 cup loosely packed fresh basil leaves
2 tablespoons parsley sprigs
1 clove garlic, peeled
1/3 cup crunchy peanut butter
1/4 cup peanut oil

3 large French or sourdough rolls, halved
12 thin slices prosciutto
12 thin slices Gouda cheese
2 tablespoons grated Parmesan cheese
2 green onions, thinly sliced

In a food processor or blender, combine basil, parsley, garlic, peanut butter and oil. Blend until finely chopped. Spread half of pesto mixture on cut sides of rolls. Arrange 2 slices of prosciutto and cheese on each half roll. Top each with remaining basil mixture. Sprinkle with Parmesan cheese and green onions. Makes 6 open-face sandwiches.

Tortilla Sandwiches

Serve tortilla sandwiches whole or cut each into wedges for easier eating.

1/2 cup crunchy peanut butter
8 (6-inch) flour tortillas
1/4 cup chutney (syrup and pieces of fruit)
4 teaspoons sweet hot or Dijon mustard
2 tablespoons vegetable oil

Spread about 2 tablespoons peanut butter on one side of four tortillas. Finely chop pieces of fruit in chutney and add back to liquid. Top peanut butter with about 1 tablespoon chutney. Spread 1 teaspoon mustard over chutney on each tortilla. Top with a second tortilla. Heat oil on a large griddle or skillet over medium heat. Add tortilla sandwiches and cook until browned on both sides, turning once. Serve warm. Makes 4 sandwiches.

Sweet & Smoky Sandwiches

*The smoky slices of Canadian bacon lend an appealing contrast to the peanut butter
and seasonings in these hearty sandwiches.*

1 teaspoon vegetable oil
12 slices (about 12 oz.) Canadian bacon
1/3 cup crunchy peanut butter
1/4 cup orange marmalade
2 (6-inch) French rolls, halved and warmed
1 tablespoon Dijon mustard
1/4 cup mayonnaise
Chopped chives

Heat oil in a 10-inch skillet over medium heat.. Add Canadian bacon and cook several minutes or until hot and starting to brown. Meanwhile, combine peanut butter and marmalade in a small bowl. Spread on cut sides of each roll. Top each with 3 slices Canadian bacon. Combine mustard and mayonnaise in a small bowl. Spread over bacon. Sprinkle with chopped chives. Makes 4 open-face sandwiches.

Monte Cristo Sandwiches

Peanut butter and chutney add new flavors to an old favorite.

1/4 cup crunchy peanut butter
1 tablespoon fruit chutney, finely chopped
2 teaspoons Dijon mustard
4 slices sandwich bread, crusts removed
4 small or 2 large slices (about 4 oz.) cooked turkey

2 small or 1 large slice (about 2 oz.) cooked ham
2 eggs, beaten slightly
1/4 cup milk
1/8 teaspoon salt
2 tablespoons vegetable oil

In a small bowl, combine peanut butter, chutney and mustard. Spread on one side of each bread slice. Arrange turkey and ham on peanut butter mixture side of 2 bread slices. Top with remaining 2 slices bread, peanut butter mixture side down. Secure with wooden picks.

In a shallow bowl, combine eggs, milk and salt. Heat oil in a 10-inch skillet over medium heat. Dip both sides of each sandwich into egg mixture. Cook until underside is golden, turn and cook remaining side until golden. Remove wooden picks. Cut each sandwich diagonally into 2 triangles. Serve warm. Makes 2 servings.

Touch-of-the-Tropics Party Sandwiches

Cut this popular snack into smaller squares or triangles for a special party appetizer.

1 (8-oz.) can crushed pineapple, well drained (see Note, page 9)
1/2 cup crunchy peanut butter
1 (8-oz.) package Neufchâtel or cream cheese, softened
1 tablespoon finely chopped candied ginger
1/2 teaspoon grated orange peel
10 slices raisin or date bread
Coarsely chopped peanuts

In a small bowl, combine pineapple, peanut butter, cheese, ginger and orange peel. Spread about 3 tablespoons mixture on each slice of bread. Sprinkle with peanuts. Makes 10 open-face sandwiches.

Variation

For tea sandwiches, cut each sandwich into quarters.

Old South Peanut Soup

Peanuts have been popular in the South since Thomas Jefferson's time.
This kind of soup has been a favorite for generations.

1 small onion, chopped
1 stalk celery, chopped
3 tablespoons margarine or butter
1/4 cup all-purpose flour

4 cups chicken broth
1 cup peanut butter
1 cup half and half or milk
Chopped peanuts

Combine onion, celery and margarine or butter in a 3-quart pan. Cook over medium heat about 10 minutes. Stir in flour and gradually stir in broth. Bring to a boil. Reduce heat and simmer about 15 minutes. Add peanut butter. Puree mixture in food processor or blender. Return mixture to pan. Stir in half and half and heat over low heat to desired temperature. Serve in soup bowls. Sprinkle with chopped peanuts. Makes about 5 or 6 cups.

Sunshine Onion Soup

A bright colorful change from traditional onion soup.

1/4 cup margarine or butter
4 medium onions, thinly sliced
1/8 teaspoon ground turmeric
1/4 teaspoon ground coriander

1/2 cup crunchy peanut butter
2 tablespoons all-purpose flour
4 cups chicken broth
Croutons (optional)

In a 3- to 4-quart pan, melt margarine or butter over medium-low heat. Add onions and cook, stirring occasionally, about 15 minutes or until onions are limp. Stir in turmeric, coriander and peanut butter, then flour. Gradually stir in chicken broth. Bring to a boil; reduce heat. Simmer, stirring occasionally, about 5 minutes or until slightly thickened. Sprinkle with croutons, if desired. Makes 4 or 5 servings.

Peanut Butter & Bacon Soup

The smoky flavor of bacon brings out the aroma and taste of the peanut butter.

4 slices bacon, chopped
1 onion, chopped
2 carrots, peeled and finely chopped
1/4 cup all-purpose flour
1/4 cup peanut butter

1 tablespoon chopped parsley
1 teaspoon chopped fresh thyme or 1/2 teaspoon
   dried thyme
1/8 teaspoon pepper
4 cups chicken broth
1 cup half and half or milk

Cook bacon in a 3-quart pan until crisp. Stir in onion and carrots, then flour. Cook, stirring occasionally, about 5 minutes. Stir in peanut butter, parsley, thyme and pepper, then broth and bring to a boil. Reduce heat and simmer, covered, 35 to 40 minutes. Puree mixture in a blender or food processor. Return mixture to pan. Stir in half and half and heat over low heat to desired temperature. Makes 4 or 5 servings.

Midas Touch Soup

This country-style soup is hearty enough to use as a luncheon main dish.

2 large sweet potatoes, peeled and cubed
1 large apple, peeled and cubed
1 onion, coarsely chopped
3 cups chicken broth or bouillon
1/2 teaspoon salt
1/8 teaspoon pepper
1 teaspoon curry powder
1/2 cup peanut butter
1/2 cup half and half or milk
Chopped peanuts

In a large saucepan, combine sweet potatoes, apple, onion, broth, salt, pepper and curry powder. Bring to a boil. Reduce heat and simmer, covered, about 20 minutes or until vegetables are tender. Add peanut butter. Puree half of mixture at a time in a blender or food processor. Return mixture to pan. Stir in half and half and heat over low heat to desired temperature. Pour into soup bowls. Sprinkle with chopped peanuts. Makes 4 or 5 servings.

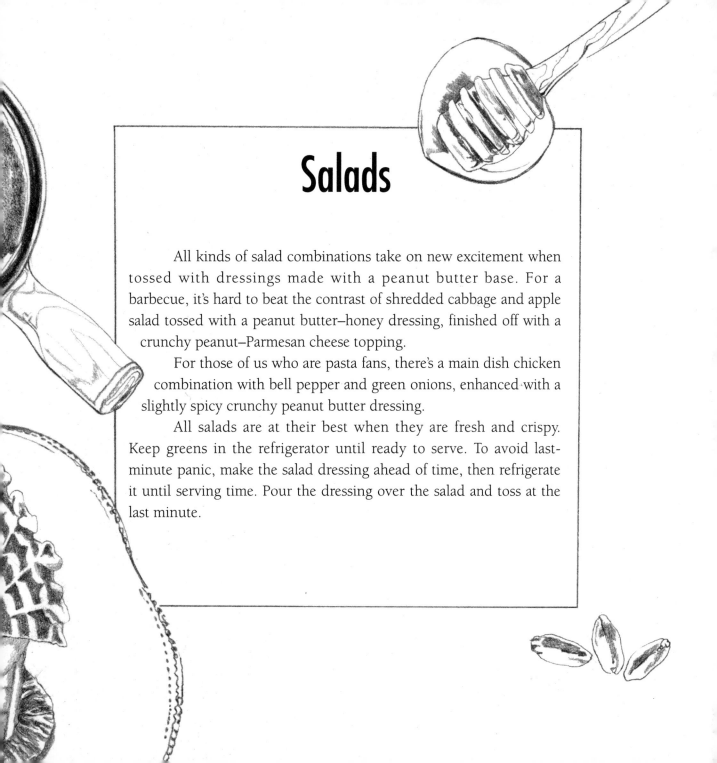

Salads

All kinds of salad combinations take on new excitement when tossed with dressings made with a peanut butter base. For a barbecue, it's hard to beat the contrast of shredded cabbage and apple salad tossed with a peanut butter–honey dressing, finished off with a crunchy peanut–Parmesan cheese topping.

For those of us who are pasta fans, there's a main dish chicken combination with bell pepper and green onions, enhanced with a slightly spicy crunchy peanut butter dressing.

All salads are at their best when they are fresh and crispy. Keep greens in the refrigerator until ready to serve. To avoid last-minute panic, make the salad dressing ahead of time, then refrigerate it until serving time. Pour the dressing over the salad and toss at the last minute.

Pasta Peanut Salad

A main-dish salad with a hearty pasta base accented with colorful vegetables.

2 cups cooked boneless chicken or pork, cut into 1-inch strips
1 medium red or yellow bell pepper, cut into 1-inch strips
1 medium zucchini, thinly sliced crosswise
2 green onions, cut into 1/2-inch pieces
8 oz. medium or small shell-shaped pasta
2/3 cup crunchy peanut butter
2/3 cup chicken broth
1 clove garlic, peeled
3 tablespoons soy sauce
1/4 teaspoon dried red pepper flakes
Carrot curls (see Note)

In a medium bowl, combine chicken or pork, bell pepper, zucchini and green onions; set aside. Cook pasta according to package directions; drain and cool.

In a blender or food processor, combine peanut butter, broth, garlic, soy sauce and pepper flakes. Process until blended. Combine chicken-vegetable mixture and cooked pasta. Pour sauce over all; toss to coat with dressing. Garnish with carrot curls. Makes 5 or 6 servings.

Note

To make carrot curls, use a vegetable peeler to cut peeled carrots into thin lengthwise strips. Roll up strips of carrot and secure rolls with wooden picks. Immerse in to a bowl of cold water and refrigerate several hours or overnight. Drain and remove wooden picks before using.

Thai-Style Platter

Enticing aromas combine with some of our favorite foods to produce a healthy dish.

3 oz. cellophane noodles
4 boneless, skinless chicken breast halves, cooked (see page 12)
2 medium zucchini, shredded
2 medium carrots, shredded
Peanutty Dressing (see below)
2 green onions, thinly sliced

Peanutty Dressing

1/3 cup crunchy peanut butter
1/4 cup soy sauce
1/4 cup lemon juice
2 tablespoons vegetable oil
1 clove garlic, chopped
2 tablespoons honey
1 1/2 teaspoons chili oil

Place noodles in a heatproof bowl; add boiling water to cover; let stand 10 to 15 minutes. Cut cooked chicken into small slivers about 1/8 x 1 inch. In a large bowl, combine chicken with zucchini and carrots. Drain noodles; arrange on a platter. Prepare dressing. Pour dressing over chicken and vegetable mixture; toss to coat. Spoon mixture over cooked noodles. Sprinkle with green onions. Makes 4 or 5 servings.

Peanutty Dressing

Combine all ingredients in a blender; process until well blended.

Crunchy Chicken Salad Bowl

This salad is at its crunchy best when served as soon as it is tossed with the dressing.

3 cups diced cooked chicken or turkey
1 cup seedless grapes, halved
1 nectarine, pitted and chopped
2 oranges, peeled and cut into chunks
1 (8-oz.) can water chestnuts, drained and sliced
1/2 cup mayonnaise
1/3 cup crunchy peanut butter
1 tablespoon finely chopped candied ginger
1/2 cup plain low-fat yogurt
1 tablespoon freshly squeezed lemon juice
2 teaspoons sesame oil
1 tablespoon soy sauce
1 cup chow mein noodles

In a large bowl, combine chicken or turkey, grapes, nectarine, oranges and water chestnuts. In a small bowl, mix together mayonnaise and peanut butter. Add ginger, yogurt, lemon juice, sesame oil and soy sauce. Pour over chicken mixture; toss to coat with dressing. Just before serving, sprinkle with chow mein noodles. Makes 5 or 6 servings.

Fruited Rice Plate

Serve with sourdough rolls and iced tea for a summer luncheon.

1 cup uncooked long-grain rice
1 teaspoon curry powder
2 cups chicken broth or bouillon
2 tablespoons boiling water
1/2 cup crunchy peanut butter
2/3 cup mayonnaise
2 green onions, thinly sliced
1 cup seedless green grapes, halved
1 mango, peeled, seeded and chopped
1 apple, chopped
2 cups cooked diced chicken or turkey
10 to 12 large lettuce leaves
2 tablespoons coarsely chopped peanuts

Combine rice, curry powder and broth or bouillon in a medium-heavy saucepan and bring to a boil. Reduce heat to low and cook, covered, 15 to 20 minutes or until tender; cool. In a small bowl, stir boiling water and peanut butter until blended; cool slightly. Stir in mayonnaise and set aside. In a large bowl, combine cooled rice, sliced green onions, grapes, mango, apple and chicken or turkey. Add dressing; toss to coat with dressing. Line plates with lettuce. Top with rice mixture. Sprinkle with chopped peanuts. Makes 5 or 6 main dish servings.

Crunchy Peanut Cole Slaw

This slaw is popular accompaniment to barbecued chicken or ribs.

2 cups shredded cabbage
1 cup coarsely chopped broccoflower or cauliflower
1 large carrot, shredded
1 tablespoon chopped chives
1 red apple, cored and chopped
2 tablespoons honey
1/4 cup crunchy peanut butter
2 tablespoons white wine vinegar
1/2 cup plain low-fat yogurt

Peanut Topping

1 tablespoon margarine or butter
1/4 cup coarsely chopped peanuts
1 tablespoon grated Parmesan cheese

Combine cabbage, broccoflower, carrot, chives and apple in a large bowl; set aside. In a small bowl, combine honey and peanut butter; stir until blended. Whisk in vinegar and yogurt. Pour dressing over cabbage mixture and toss until coated with dressing. Prepare Peanut Topping and cool slightly until warm. Sprinkle Peanut topping over cole slaw. Makes 4 to 6 servings.

Peanut Topping

Melt margarine in a small skillet over medium heat; stir in peanuts. Cook, stirring, about three minutes or until peanuts start to brown. Remove from heat; stir in Parmesan cheese.

Peanut Waldorf Slaw

This nostalgic salad is at its best when served as soon as it is made.

1/4 cup crunchy peanut butter
1/4 cup mayonnaise
1/4 cup plain low-fat yogurt
1 tablespoon honey
1 teaspoon freshly squeezed lemon juice
4 cups shredded Chinese cabbage
1 apple, diced
1/2 cup red or green seedless grapes, halved if large
1/4 cup peanuts

In a small bowl, combine peanut butter, mayonnaise, yogurt, honey and lemon juice; set aside. In a large salad bowl, combine shredded cabbage, apple and grapes. Add salad dressing; toss until coated with dressing. Top with peanuts. Makes 4 to 6 servings.

Year-Round Fresh Fruit Salad

Use these popular fruits for the basic salad, then add a favorite seasonal one, when available.

2 apples, diced
2 oranges, peeled and cut into chunks
1 banana, peeled and sliced crosswise
1 tablespoon honey
1/4 cup crunchy peanut butter
1/2 cup plain low-fat yogurt
1/3 cup golden raisins (optional)
Chopped peanuts

Combine apples, oranges and banana in a large bowl; set aside. In a small bowl, stir honey and peanut butter until well mixed. Add yogurt and raisins, if desired. Spoon over fruits. Toss until well blended. Sprinkle with chopped peanuts. Makes 4 or 5 servings.

Taste-of-the-South-Seas Fruit Compote

Chop the remaining pineapple and freeze it in a heavy plastic bag to add to fruit drinks or a fruit salad.

1/4 cup peanut butter
2 tablespoons honey
2 tablespoons orange juice
1/2 teaspoon grated gingerroot
1/4 teaspoon grated orange peel
1/4 cup orange yogurt
1 papaya or mango, peeled, seeded or pitted, and cut into bite-size pieces
2 bananas, peeled and cut crosswise into thick slices
1/2 fresh pineapple, peeled and cut into chunks
Coarsely chopped peanuts

In a small bowl, combine peanut butter and honey and stir until blended. Add orange juice, gingerroot and orange peel. Stir in yogurt. In a medium bowl, combine papaya or mango, bananas and pineapple. Toss with dressing. Sprinkle with coarsely chopped peanuts. Makes about 6 servings.

Variation

If good fresh pineapple is not available, use 1 (16-oz.) can pineapple chunks, drained.

Summertime Fruit Treat

Take advantage of fresh summer fruits in this colorful first course or dessert.

1/4 cup mango chutney
1/3 cup peanut butter
1/4 cup orange juice
1/2 teaspoon ground ginger
1 small honeydew or cantaloupe, peeled, seeded and diced
1 banana, peeled and sliced crosswise
2 cups fresh raspberries or sweet cherries, halved and pitted

Finely chop fruit in chutney and return to liquid. In a medium bowl, combine peanut butter and chutney and stir until combined. Stir in orange juice and ginger; set aside. In a large bowl, combine honeydew or cantaloupe, banana and raspberries or cherries. Spoon into individual sherbet glasses. Spoon peanut butter topping over each. Makes 7 or 8 servings.

Tropical Peanut Butter Dressing

This light and slightly sweet dressing will enhance your favorite fruit salad combinations.

1/4 cup crunchy peanut butter
2 tablespoons vegetable oil
1 teaspoon minced chives
1 tablespoon minced candied ginger
1/2 cup apricot-pineapple or orange yogurt

Combine peanut butter, oil, chives and ginger. Gradually stir in yogurt. Makes about 3/4 cup.

Main Dishes

You may not think of peanut butter as an important ingredient in main dishes. However, there is a wide variety of main dishes throughout the world that use peanut butter in savory sauces and in the dishes themselves. Americans discovered the spicy satés and curries from Southeast Asia and the Orient. Then we adapted these dishes for use with our popular chicken and turkey products as well as with pork and seafood. The result is an exciting new group of main dishes featuring peanut butter.

If you have not tried one of these combinations, start your family with one that includes some flavors that they enjoy and with which they are familiar. Then progress to some of the more exotic flavor medleys.

A bed of cooked rice or noodles provides a welcome contrast to many of these ethnic dishes.

Pork Loin with Apple–Peanut Butter Sauce

For convenience, marinate the pork in a large heavy plastic bag.
It can be left in the refrigerator up to 24 hours before cooking.

1 1/2 to 2 lbs. boneless pork loin roast
1/4 cup maple syrup
2 tablespoons freshly squeezed lemon juice
1 teaspoon ground ginger
1/2 teaspoon freshly grated nutmeg
1/4 teaspoon salt
1/8 teaspoon pepper
1 tablespoon vegetable oil
1/3 cup crunchy peanut butter
2 apples, peeled and chopped
1 orange, peeled and sliced

Place pork in a large self-sealing plastic bag. Add maple syrup, lemon juice, ginger, nutmeg, salt, pepper and oil. Close bag; refrigerate at least 2 hours, turning occasionally.

Preheat oven to 350°F (175°C). Remove pork from marinade, reserving marinade. Place pork in a small baking pan and roast about 1 1/4 hours or until internal temperature reaches 160°F to 170°F (70°C to 75°C). Remove from oven and let rest about 20 minutes before slicing.

Meanwhile, pour marinade into a small saucepan. Add peanut butter and apples and bring to a boil. Reduce heat, cover and cook over low heat 15 to 20 minutes or until apples are tender. Slice cooked pork loin. Spoon sauce with apples over pork. Garnish with orange slices. Makes 6 to 8 servings.

Javanese Chicken Kebabs

Hot cooked rice is an excellent complement to these typical chicken kebabs.

1/4 cup peanut butter
2 tablespoons honey
1 clove garlic, peeled
1 teaspoon grated gingerroot
2 tablespoons soy sauce
Several dashes bottled hot pepper sauce
1 tablespoon sesame oil
1 lb. boneless, skinless chicken breasts, cut into 3/4-inch chunks
30 small fresh mushrooms
Sliced mangoes

In a blender or food processor, process peanut butter, honey, garlic, ginger, soy sauce, hot pepper sauce and sesame oil until combined. Thread each metal skewer with 4 chicken cubes and 3 mushrooms, beginning with a chicken cube and alternating with mushrooms. Preheat broiler or grill. Broil or grill kebabs about 15 minutes, turning and brushing several times with peanut butter mixture. Garnish with mango slices. Makes 4 or 5 servings.

 Note

If using wooden or bamboo skewers, soak them in water 30 minutes before using to prevent their burning during cooking.

Turkey & Peanut Butter Enchiladas

These are not your traditional enchiladas.
The peanut butter and honey add a sweet richness to the spicy sauce.

2/3 cup crunchy peanut butter
3 tablespoons honey
2 tablespoons soy sauce
2 tablespoons freshly squeezed lemon juice
1 tablespoon grated gingerroot
2 1/2 cups bottled picante sauce
2 cups diced cooked turkey or chicken
3 green onions, thinly sliced
4 mushrooms, thinly sliced
8 corn tortillas
1/4 cup chopped peanuts
Dairy sour cream (optional)
Shredded lettuce (optional)

Preheat oven to 350°F (175°C). In a medium saucepan, combine peanut butter, honey, soy sauce and lemon juice; cook, stirring, until blended. Add gingerroot and picante sauce. Set aside about 1 1/2 cups of the mixture. Stir turkey or chicken, green onions and mushrooms into remaining sauce. Spoon about 1/3 cup turkey mixture down center of each tortilla, roll up and place seam side down in a 13 x 9-inch baking dish. Spoon reserved sauce over top. Sprinkle with peanuts. Bake 15 to 20 minutes or until bubbly. Top with sour cream and shredded lettuce, if desired. Makes 8 servings.

Pork Saté Kebabs

This dish can also be served as part of an appetizer selection.
Tropical fruits would add interesting flavor contrasts.

1 tablespoon vegetable oil
1 clove garlic, crushed
1 medium tomato, peeled, seeded and chopped
1/3 cup crunchy peanut butter
1 cup chicken broth or bouillon
1/4 teaspoon dried red pepper flakes
1 lb. boneless pork tenderloin, cut into 1-inch cubes

Heat oil and garlic in a small saucepan over medium heat. Stir in tomato, peanut butter, broth and pepper flakes. Simmer 5 minutes; set aside. Thread 6-inch skewers with 4 or 5 cubes of pork and place in a 12 x 7-inch baking pan. Pour tomato mixture over kebabs, cover and refrigerate 4 to 6 hours.

Preheat broiler or grill. Brush pork with marinade and grill about 4 inches from heat source 7 minutes. Turn and grill 5 minutes. Makes 5 or 6 servings.

African-Style Vegetables & Rice

This change-of-pace hearty main dish blends a variety of flavors.
You will be surprised at how delicious the sweet potato is.

1 tablespoon vegetable oil
1 red onion, chopped
1 clove garlic, crushed
1 green or yellow bell pepper, cored, seeded and chopped
1 cup uncooked long-grain white rice
1 small sweet potato, peeled and chopped into 1/2-inch pieces
1 (13- to 14-oz.) can pinto beans, drained
4 cups chicken broth
1 (16-oz.) jar salsa
1/2 teaspoon dried oregano leaves
1/2 cup peanut butter
Sour cream or yogurt

In a 4-quart saucepan, heat oil over medium heat. Add onion and garlic; cook, stirring occasionally, about 5 minutes or until onion is softened. Stir in bell pepper, rice, sweet potato, pinto beans, broth, 1 1/2 cups of the salsa and oregano leaves. Bring to a boil. Reduce heat, cover and cook over low heat 25 to 35 minutes or until sweet potato and rice are tender. Stir in peanut butter. Top with sour cream or yogurt and remaining 1/2 cup salsa. Makes 8 servings.

Pasta & Turkey Toss with Snow Peas

Noodles with a peanut butter sauce is a wonderful change from traditional pasta dishes.

6 oz. corkscrew pasta (about 2 1/4 cups uncooked)
2/3 cup chicken broth
1/2 cup peanut butter
1 clove garlic, peeled
2 green onions, cut into 1-inch pieces
1/4 teaspoon red pepper flakes
2 tablespoons soy sauce
2 cups chopped cooked turkey or chicken
1/2 cup snow peas
2 tablespoons dry white wine
Papaya or nectarine cubes

Cook pasta according to package directions; drain. While pasta cooks, combine broth, peanut butter, garlic, onions, pepper flakes and soy sauce in a blender or food processor. Blend until onions are finely chopped.

   In a large skillet, combine turkey or chicken, pureed peanut butter mixture, cooked drained pasta, snow peas and wine. Heat and stir over medium heat until combined and heated through. Garnish with papaya or nectarine cubes. Makes 4 to 6 servings.

Gingered Orange Pork

Serve pork on a large platter or on individual plates over cooked rice or noodles.

1 tablespoon vegetable oil
6 boneless pork cutlets or chops, about 1/2 inch thick
2 tablespoons cornstarch
1 1/2 cups chicken broth or bouillon
1/4 cup crunchy peanut butter
2 teaspoons grated gingerroot
1/4 teaspoon salt
1 (11-oz.) can mandarin oranges, drained
1 (8-oz.) can sliced water chestnuts, drained
1 cup fresh or frozen snow peas

Heat vegetable oil in a large skillet over medium heat. Add pork. Cook 4 to 5 minutes on each side or until no longer pink in center and lightly browned. Remove from skillet; keep warm.

Dissolve cornstarch in broth or bouillon. Stir into drippings in skillet. Add peanut butter. Cook and stir over medium heat until thickened. Add gingerroot, salt, oranges, water chestnuts and snow peas. Cook, stirring occasionally, until hot. Spoon vegetables and sauce over cooked pork. Makes 6 servings.

Teriyaki Shrimp & Vegetable Pizza

An exciting and easy new pizza topped with shrimp and teriyaki sauce.

1 (10-oz.) thin pizza crust, such as Boboli
1 tablespoon vegetable oil
2 medium carrots, peeled and shredded
1 medium onion, thinly sliced
8 to 10 medium mushrooms, thinly sliced
1 cup fresh bean sprouts (about 3 oz.)
1/4 lb. cooked, shelled small shrimp
1/2 cup crunchy peanut butter
2 tablespoons teriyaki sauce
1 clove garlic, crushed
1/3 cup orange juice
1 teaspoon chili powder
1 tablespoon finely chopped cilantro

Preheat oven to 425°F (220°C). Place crust on a baking sheet. Heat oil in a small skillet over medium heat. Add carrots and onion and cook, stirring occasionally, 4 to 5 minutes or until vegetables are softened. Add mushrooms; cook 1 minute. Sprinkle cooked vegetables and bean sprouts over crust. Top with shrimp.

In a small bowl, combine peanut butter, teriyaki sauce, garlic, orange juice and chili powder. Spoon over shrimp mixture on crust. Bake about 10 minutes or until topping is hot. Sprinkle with cilantro. Cut into wedges. Makes 5 or 6 servings.

Curried Mango Chicken with Balinese Sauce

Accompany the chicken with steamed white rice and broccoli.

2 tablespoons freshly squeezed lemon juice
1 tablespoon honey
1 teaspoon curry powder
1/2 teaspoon Dijon mustard
1 clove garlic, crushed
1/4 cup vegetable oil
1/4 teaspoon salt
1/8 teaspoon pepper
6 boneless, skinless chicken breast halves or thighs
Balinese Sauce (see below)

Balinese Sauce

1/3 cup mango chutney
1/3 cup crunchy peanut butter

Combine lemon juice, honey, curry powder, mustard, garlic, oil, salt and pepper in a small bowl. Pour marinade over chicken; cover and refrigerate 3 or 4 hours.

Preheat broiler or grill. Remove chicken from marinade and cook about 5 inches from heat about 8 minutes on each side or until cooked through. Meanwhile prepare sauce. Spread sauce over grilled chicken. Makes 6 servings.

Balinese Sauce

Coarsely chop any pieces of fruit in chutney and return to liquid. Combine chutney with peanut butter.

Saté-Style Pizza

Start with a prepared pizza crust; enhance it with exotic, flavorful toppings.

1 tablespoon vegetable oil
1 clove garlic, crushed
2 cups (1/2-inch cubes) boneless ham
2/3 cup crunchy peanut butter
2 tablespoons soy sauce
1 teaspoon Dijon mustard
1/2 cup chicken broth
1 tablespoon honey
1 teaspoon grated gingerroot
1 (11 1/2- to 12-inch) baked pizza crust
1 small red or yellow bell pepper, thinly sliced into strips
1/2 cup canned pineapple chunks, well drained
1/2 cup snow peas, halved
2 green onions, thinly sliced

Preheat oven to 400°F (205°C). In a 10-inch skillet, heat oil. Stir in garlic, then ham. Add peanut butter, soy sauce, mustard, chicken broth, honey and gingerroot. Cook over medium heat, stirring, until combined, about 5 minutes.

Place crust on a baking sheet. Top with bell pepper, pineapple and snow peas. Spoon cooked mixture over all. Sprinkle with onions. Bake about 12 minutes or until topping is hot. Makes 4 or 5 servings.

Chicken–Peanut Butter Tostada

For a special treat, top finished tostada with a dab of plain unflavored yogurt or sour cream.

1/2 cup crunchy peanut butter
2 tablespoons soy sauce
1 clove garlic, crushed
1 tablespoon sweet hot mustard
1/4 teaspoon red pepper flakes
1/2 cup chicken broth or bouillon
2 cups chopped cooked chicken
2 tablespoons vegetable oil
4 flour tortillas
3 cups shredded lettuce
1 large tomato, chopped
2 green onions, sliced
2 tablespoons chopped cilantro

In a medium saucepan, combine peanut butter, soy sauce, garlic, mustard, pepper flakes and broth or bouillon. Cook and stir over low heat until peanut butter melts. Stir in cooked chicken; set aside.

In a large skillet or griddle, heat oil. Cook tortillas on both sides until crispy and a light golden color; drain on paper towels. Spoon about 1/2 cup chicken mixture on to each crisp tortilla. Top with lettuce, tomato, green onions and cilantro. Makes 4 servings.

Touch-of-the-Orient Pasta

Start a new trend by serving this exciting cold pasta dish for an easy lunch.

8 oz. angel hair pasta
1 tablespoon sesame oil
1/3 cup peanut butter
1 tablespoon white wine vinegar
1 tablespoon honey
1 tablespoon hoisin sauce
1/2 teaspoon grated gingerroot
1/4 teaspoon red pepper flakes
1 tablespoon chopped cilantro
1/3 cup chicken broth or bouillon
1 tablespoon sesame seeds, toasted

Cook pasta according to package directions; drain and rinse. Place in a large bowl and toss with oil; set aside. In a small bowl, combine peanut butter, vinegar, honey, hoisin sauce, gingerroot, pepper flakes and cilantro. Stir in broth. Pour over pasta; toss until well coated. Sprinkle with toasted sesame seeds. Makes 5 or 6 servings.

Variation

Add chunks of cooked chicken to the noodles before adding the sauce.

Thai Pork Stir-fry

Use your favorite large heavy skillet or a wok over very hot heat,
then stir constantly to cook ingredients evenly.

1/3 cup peanut butter
1 tablespoon sesame oil
3 tablespoons hoisin sauce
3 tablespoons white wine vinegar
1/4 teaspoon dried red pepper flakes
1 clove garlic, crushed
2 tablespoons vegetable oil
1 (3/4-lb.) pork tenderloin, cut into small strips
2 crookneck squash, thinly sliced
2 zucchini, thinly sliced
1 cup sugar snap peas
2 green onions, sliced
1 (8-oz.) can sliced water chestnuts, drained
2 tablespoons chopped peanuts

In a small saucepan, whisk together peanut butter and sesame oil. Gradually add hoisin sauce, whisking until smooth. Stir in vinegar, pepper flakes and garlic; set aside.

In a 12-inch skillet, heat vegetable oil over high heat. Add pork and cook, stirring constantly, about 10 minutes or until pork is browned. Remove pork from skillet. Add crookneck squash and zucchini to skillet. Cook, stirring constantly, 3 to 4 minutes or until tender. Add peas, green onions, water chestnuts, cooked pork and reserved sauce. Stir until well mixed. Sprinkle with chopped peanuts. Makes 4 or 5 servings.

Malaysian Chicken Kebabs

The flavor secret is to marinate the chicken, then brush it with the marinade at least once while cooking.

1/3 cup crunchy peanut butter
1 tablespoon honey
1 clove garlic, crushed
1 tablespoon freshly squeezed lemon juice
2 tablespoons soy sauce
1/4 teaspoon ground coriander
1/8 teaspoon ground red (cayenne) pepper
1/2 teaspoon grated gingerroot
1/2 teaspoon salt
1 1/4 lbs. boneless, skinless chicken breasts, cut into 1 1/2-inch pieces

In a small bowl, stir together peanut butter and honey. Add garlic, lemon juice, soy sauce, coriander, cayenne, ginger and salt. Thread chicken pieces on 8- to 10-inch skewers. Brush evenly with marinade, cover and refrigerate at least 2 hours.

Preheat broiler or grill. Cook kebabs about 5 inches from heat source about 5 minutes. Turn, brush with sauce and cook 4 minutes longer or until chicken is browned and cooked through. Makes 6 skewers.

Turkey & Green Chile Pasta

This popular pasta dish is topped with a spicy turkey mixture.

8 oz. small spiral pasta
12 to 16 oz. boneless, skinless turkey breast
2 tablespoons vegetable oil
1 clove garlic, crushed
1/4 cup crunchy peanut butter
1 tablespoon honey
1 tablespoon soy sauce
1 tablespoon hoisin sauce
1/4 cup orange juice
1 green chile, seeded and finely chopped
1 cup chicken broth
2 tablespoons cornstarch mixed with 1 tablespoon white wine
1 tablespoon chopped cilantro

Cook pasta according to package directions; drain. Rinse with hot water; drain and set aside.

While pasta cooks, cut turkey into small strips. Heat oil and garlic in a large skillet over medium heat. Add turkey and cook, stirring, until turkey is white, about 10 minutes. Stir in peanut butter and honey. Add soy sauce, hoisin sauce, orange juice, chile, chicken broth and cornstarch mixture and bring to a boil. Reduce heat, cover and simmer, stirring occasionally, 5 to 6 minutes or until turkey is tender. Arrange pasta on a large platter; top with turkey and sauce. Sprinkle with cilantro. Makes 4 or 5 servings.

Creamy Macaroni & Peas with Peanut Butter

Not the usual macaroni and cheese, this dish may become the new family favorite.

8 oz. uncooked macaroni
2 tablespoons margarine or butter
1/2 teaspoon salt
1/8 teaspoon pepper
1/4 teaspoon ground cinnamon
2 green onions, thinly sliced
2 tablespoons all-purpose flour
2 cups milk
1 (3-oz.) package cream cheese, diced
1/3 cup crunchy peanut butter
1 cup cooked green peas

Cook macaroni according to package directions; drain and set aside.

In a medium saucepan, heat margarine or butter, salt, pepper and cinnamon over low heat. Add green onions and cook, stirring occasionally, 2 to 3 minutes. Stir in flour. Slowly stir in milk. Add cream cheese and peanut butter and cook, stirring constantly, over low heat about 5 minutes or until cream cheese melts. Stir in peas and macaroni and heat through. Makes 6 to 8 servings.

Variations

If desired, stir in a bit of chopped cooked bacon or ham with the peas. Thawed frozen green peas can be used instead of cooked peas.

Breads

The fragrant aroma of freshly baked bread from Grandma's kitchen is a fond memory for me. Today, most of us still enjoy fresh-from-the-oven muffins, coffee cakes and loaves of quick breads.

There's almost an unlimited range in flavor and texture for peanut butter muffins. Peanut Butter & Jelly Muffins are designed to appeal to folks of all ages who fondly remember their childhood favorite combination.

Quick-bread treats range from the wonderful flavors in Sour Cherry Peanut Bread to a traditional Streusel Carrot Coffeecake. All of these loaves are equally delicious when served warm from the oven or as a great quick-and-easy choice for tomorrow's on-the-run breakfast or after-school treat.

Apricot Ginger Muffins

This impressive blend of ingredients results in exotic flavors.

1/3 cup peanut butter
1/2 cup vegetable oil
1 egg, beaten slightly
1 cup milk
1/2 cup finely chopped dried apricots

1/2 teaspoon grated orange peel
1 tablespoon finely chopped candied ginger
1 3/4 cups all-purpose flour
1/4 cup sugar
1/2 teaspoon baking soda

Preheat oven to 400°F (205°C). Lightly grease 12 muffin cups.

Combine peanut butter and oil in a large bowl. Stir in egg and milk. Stir in apricots, orange peel and ginger. Add flour, sugar and baking soda. Stir just until dry ingredients are moistened and mixture is still slightly lumpy. Spoon into prepared muffin cups. Bake 17 to 20 minutes or until golden. Serve hot. Makes 12 muffins.

Peanut Butter & Jelly Muffins

Traditional flavors with tooth-some goodness results in a favorite muffin.

1/3 cup crunchy peanut butter
1/4 cup sugar
1/3 cup vegetable oil
1 egg, beaten slightly
3/4 cup milk
1 3/4 cups all-purpose flour
2 1/2 teaspoons baking powder
1/4 cup grape jelly or strawberry jam

Preheat oven to 400°F (205°C). Grease 12 muffin cups or line with paper liners.

In a large bowl, combine peanut butter and sugar. Gradually stir in oil. Stir in egg and milk. Add flour and baking powder. Stir just until dry ingredients are moistened and mixture is still slightly lumpy. Spoon half of mixture into prepared muffin cups. Top each with 1 teaspoon of the jelly or jam, then the remaining batter. Bake 20 to 25 minutes or until golden.

Remove muffins from pan and cool on wire racks. Serve warm or at room temperature. Makes 12 muffins.

Honey Bran Muffins

Try these freshly baked muffins at a Sunday brunch or a special luncheon.

1 1/2 cups whole-bran cereal
1 cup buttermilk (see Note)
1 egg
1/3 cup honey
1/3 cup crunchy peanut butter

1/3 cup vegetable oil
1 1/2 cups whole-wheat flour
1 teaspoon baking soda
1/4 teaspoon salt

Preheat oven to 350°F (175°C). Grease 12 muffin cups or line with paper liners. In a small bowl, combine cereal and buttermilk; let stand 5 minutes.

In a large bowl, beat together egg, honey, peanut butter and oil. Stir in flour, baking soda and salt just until dry ingredients are moistened. Stir in cereal mixture just to combine. Spoon into prepared muffin cups. Bake 15 to 20 minutes or until muffins spring back when lightly pressed. Remove muffins from pan and cool on wire racks. Serve warm or at room temperature. Makes 12 muffins.

Note

If buttermilk is not available, add 1 teaspoon vinegar or lemon juice to measuring cup before adding regular milk. Dried buttermilk is also available in most supermarkets.

Chocolate Peanut Butter Muffins

This quick and easy muffin results in the all-time favorite combination.

1/4 cup margarine or butter
1/3 cup peanut butter
3/4 cup sugar
1 egg
1/2 cup milk
1 cup all-purpose flour
1/3 cup unsweetened cocoa powder
2 teaspoons baking powder

Preheat oven to 400°F (205°C). Line muffin cups with paper liners. In a large mixing bowl, beat margarine or butter with peanut butter and sugar until light and fluffy. Beat in egg and milk. Stir in flour, cocoa powder and baking powder. Spoon into prepared muffin cups. Bake 20 to 25 minutes.

Remove muffins from pan and cool on wire racks. Serve warm or at room temperature. Makes 12 muffins.

Peanut Butter Banana Muffins

The blend of peanut butter and banana flavors results in a just-right moist texture.

1/2 cup lightly packed brown sugar
1/3 cup solid vegetable shortening
1/3 cup crunchy peanut butter
2 eggs
3/4 cup mashed ripe bananas (about 2 medium bananas)
1/3 cup milk
1 teaspoon baking powder
1/2 teaspoon baking soda
2 cups all-purpose flour

Preheat oven to 400°F (205°C). Grease or line 12 muffin cups with paper liners.

In a large bowl, beat brown sugar, shortening and peanut butter until light and fluffy. Beat in eggs. Mix in mashed bananas and milk. Stir in baking powder, baking soda and flour just until dry ingredients are moistened. Spoon into prepared muffin cups. Bake 20 to 25 minutes or until muffins spring back when lightly pressed.

Remove muffins from pan and cool on wire racks. Serve warm or at room temperature. Makes 12 muffins.

Savory Bacon Muffins

A special accompaniment to spicy pork dishes or tropical fruit plates.

1/3 cup peanut butter
1/4 cup vegetable oil
1 1/4 cups milk
2 eggs
1/4 teaspoon dried red pepper flakes
1 tablespoon minced green onion
2 slices bacon, cooked until crisp and crumbled
1 1/2 cups all-purpose flour
1/2 cup cornmeal
1 tablespoon baking powder

Grease or line 12 muffin cups with paper liners. Preheat oven to 400°F (205°C).

In a large bowl, beat together peanut butter and oil. Whisk in milk and eggs. Add red pepper flakes, onion and bacon. Stir in flour, cornmeal and baking powder just until dry ingredients are moistened. Spoon into prepared muffin cups. Bake 25 to 30 minutes or until muffins spring back when lightly pressed.

Remove muffins from pan and cool on wire racks. Serve warm or at room temperature. Makes 12 muffins.

Upside-Down Apricot Peanut Rolls

Peanut butter and apricots combine with spices to produce a very appealing sweet roll.

1/3 cup chopped peanuts
1/3 cup margarine or butter
1/3 cup brown sugar
2 cups biscuit baking mix
1/2 cup water
1/3 cup peanut butter
1/4 cup finely chopped dried apricots
2 tablespoons granulated sugar
1/2 teaspoon ground cinnamon
1/8 teaspoon ground allspice

Preheat oven to 400°F (205°C). Sprinkle equal amounts of peanuts into 12 muffin cups. Heat margarine or butter with brown sugar, stirring constantly, until blended. Spoon mixture over peanuts in muffin cups.

In a medium bowl, combine biscuit mix with water; mix into a soft dough. Knead until smooth on a floured board. Roll dough out into a 13 x 9-inch rectangle. Gently spread or drop small amounts of peanut butter and apricots evenly over surface of dough. In a small bowl, combine granulated sugar, cinnamon and allspice; sprinkle over peanut butter and apricots. Starting at one long side, roll up tightly like a jelly roll; pinch edges of dough to seal.

Cut roll crosswise into 12 slices. Place 1 slice in each prepared muffin cup. Bake about 15 minutes or until golden brown. Immediately invert pan onto a heatproof tray or platter. Makes 12 rolls.

Spicy Applesauce Loaf

Old-fashioned flavors of cinnamon and nutmeg with applesauce enhance this healthful loaf.

2 eggs
1/2 cup lightly packed brown sugar
1/2 cup peanut butter
1 cup milk
1 cup whole-wheat flour
1 cup all-purpose flour

1 tablespoon baking powder
1/2 teaspoon baking soda
1/2 teaspoon ground cinnamon
1/4 teaspoon freshly grated nutmeg
1/2 cup applesauce

Preheat oven to 350°F (175°C). Grease a 9-inch loaf pan.

In a large bowl, beat eggs, brown sugar and peanut butter until light and fluffy. Mix in milk, flours, baking powder, baking soda, cinnamon, nutmeg and applesauce. Spoon batter into prepared pan. Bake 45 to 50 minutes or until a wooden pick inserted in center comes out clean.

Cool loaf in pan on a wire rack 10 minutes. Invert onto rack; slice while warm or cool. Makes 1 loaf.

Sour Cherry Peanut Bread

Pour cherries into a strainer or colander and very lightly press with the back of a spoon to remove all the liquid.

1/4 cup solid vegetable shortening
3/4 cup plus 2 tablespoons sugar
1/4 cup peanut butter
2 eggs
1/2 cup buttermilk
2 cups all-purpose flour

1 teaspoon baking powder
1 teaspoon baking soda
1 (16-oz.) can pitted red tart cherries, drained
1/4 cup chopped peanuts
1/4 teaspoon ground cinnamon

Preheat oven to 350°F (175°C). Grease a 9-inch springform pan. In a large bowl, beat shortening, 3/4 cup sugar and peanut butter until light and fluffy. Add eggs and buttermilk; beat until smooth. Stir in flour, baking powder and baking soda until combined. Add cherries. Spoon batter into prepared pan.

Combine peanuts, remaining 2 tablespoons sugar and cinnamon. Sprinkle mixture over top. Bake 40 to 45 minutes until top springs back when lightly pressed with finger. Cut into 6 to 8 wedges and serve warm. Makes 6 to 8 servings.

Summer Harvest Coffeecake

Use fresh peaches for the best flavor.

2 eggs
2/3 cup granulated sugar
1/4 cup margarine or butter, melted
1/2 cup milk
1 1/3 cups all-purpose flour
2 teaspoons baking powder
2 fresh peaches, peeled, pitted and sliced
2 tablespoons peanut butter
1/3 cup lightly packed brown sugar
1/4 teaspoon freshly grated nutmeg
2 tablespoons chopped peanuts

Preheat oven to 400°F (205°C). Grease and flour a 9-inch springform pan.

In a large bowl, beat eggs and granulated sugar until light. Add margarine or butter and milk; mix well. Beat in flour and baking powder until smooth. Pour batter into prepared pan. Arrange sliced peaches on top.

In a small bowl, cut peanut butter into brown sugar and nutmeg until crumbly. Sprinkle mixture over peaches. Top with peanuts. Bake about 35 minutes or until top springs back when lightly pressed with finger. Cool in pan. Cut into wedges. Serve warm or cool. Makes 6 servings.

Streusel Carrot Coffeecake

These enticing flavor combinations will add a welcome touch to a special event.

Streusel Topping (see below)
1 1/4 cups all-purpose flour
1 cup sugar
1 teaspoon baking powder
1/4 teaspoon baking soda
1/2 teaspoon ground cinnamon
1/2 cup vegetable oil
2 eggs, slightly beaten
1 medium carrot, peeled and shredded

Streusel Topping

1/3 cup crunchy peanut butter
2/3 cup lightly packed brown sugar
2 tablespoons margarine or butter, softened
1/3 cup all-purpose flour
1/2 teaspoon freshly grated nutmeg
1/4 cup coarsely chopped peanuts

Grease a 9-inch springform pan. Prepare topping; set aside. Preheat oven to 350°F (175°C).

In a large bowl, stir together flour, sugar, baking powder, baking soda and cinnamon. Add oil, eggs and carrot. Beat with an electric mixer at medium speed 2 minutes. Spoon batter into prepared pan. Spoon topping over top. Bake about 35 minutes or until edges begin to pull away.

Cool cake on a wire rack about 5 minutes. Remove springform ring, cut into wedges and serve warm. Makes 6 to 8 servings.

Streusel Topping

In a small bowl, combine peanut butter with remaining ingredients until crumbly.

Oasis Coffeecake

Rich and creamy coffeecake is enhanced by a combination of dates with a cinnamon-sugar mixture.

Cinnamon Sugar (see below)
1/2 cup peanut butter
1/3 cup vegetable oil
1 1/4 cups sugar
2 eggs
1 teaspoon vanilla extract
2 cups all-purpose flour
2 teaspoons baking powder
1/2 teaspoon baking soda
1 cup dairy sour cream
1/2 cup chopped dates

Cinnamon Sugar

2 tablespoons sugar
1/2 teaspoon ground cinnamon

Preheat oven to 350°F (175°C). Grease and flour a 10-inch tube pan. Prepare Cinnamon Sugar; set aside.

In a large bowl, beat peanut butter, oil, sugar, eggs and vanilla until combined. Add half the flour, the baking powder and baking soda and beat until smooth. Mix in sour cream, then remaining flour.

Spread half of batter into prepared pan. Top with dates and half of Cinnamon Sugar, then remaining batter. Top with remaining Cinnamon Sugar. Bake 50 minutes or until a wooden pick inserted in center comes out clean.

Cool cake in pan 10 minutes. Turn out of pan and cut into thick wedges. Makes 8 to 10 servings.

Cinnamon Sugar

In a small bowl, combine sugar and cinnamon.

Apple Brunch Wedges

An enticing accompaniment to a special brunch menu.

2/3 cup sugar
1/4 cup peanut butter
1/2 cup vegetable oil
2 eggs
1 large tart apple, peeled, cored and chopped
1/4 cup chopped peanuts
1 cup all-purpose flour
1 teaspoon baking soda
1/2 teaspoon ground allspice
1/4 teaspoon ground cardamom
1/8 teaspoon freshly grated nutmeg
Easy Glaze (see below)

Easy Glaze

2 tablespoons margarine or butter, melted
1 cup powdered sugar, sifted
2 tablespoons milk

Grease an 8- or 9-inch round cake pan. Preheat oven to 350°F (175°C).

In a large bowl, combine sugar, peanut butter and oil. Beat in eggs until blended. Stir in apple and peanuts. Stir in flour, baking soda, allspice, cardamom and nutmeg. Spoon batter into prepared pan. Bake about 25 minutes or until top is lightly browned.

Cool cake in pan 10 minutes. Turn out of pan and cool on a wire rack.

While cake is cooling, prepare glaze. Spread over top of cooled cake. Cut into small wedges. Makes 5 or 6 servings.

Easy Glaze

In a small bowl, stir together margarine or butter, powdered sugar and milk until smooth.

Orange Maple French Toast

A special treat for a lazy Sunday morning or holiday.

4 eggs
1 tablespoon sugar
1/4 teaspoon grated orange peel
1 cup orange juice
1 cup half and half or milk
8 1-inch-thick slices French bread
Peanut Maple Sauce (see below)
1/4 cup margarine or butter

Peanut Maple Sauce

1/2 cup crunchy peanut butter
1/2 cup maple syrup
1/2 teaspoon ground cinnamon

In a medium bowl, beat eggs with sugar. Stir in orange peel, orange juice and half and half or milk. Pour into a 13 x 9-inch baking dish. Add bread. Cover and refrigerate at least 3 hours or overnight, turning bread once.

Prepare sauce and keep warm. Melt butter or margarine in a large skillet or griddle over medium heat. Add soaked bread. Cook 3 to 4 minutes or until golden brown. Turn and cook other side. Serve with Peanut Maple Sauce. Makes 8 servings.

Peanut Maple Sauce

In a small saucepan, combine peanut butter, maple syrup and cinnamon. Cook over low heat, stirring, until warm and peanut butter is melted.

Fruit-filled Pancakes

Tailor this treat with seasonal fruits for a special event brunch.

1/2 cup crunchy peanut butter
1 (3-oz.) package cream cheese, softened
2 eggs
1 tablespoon granulated sugar
1/4 cup all-purpose flour
1/2 cup milk
1/4 teaspoon vanilla extract
1 tablespoon margarine or butter
2 peaches, peeled and sliced
1 banana, sliced crosswise
1 kiwi fruit, peeled and thinly sliced
1 tablespoon powdered sugar
1/2 cup boysenberry or raspberry syrup

In a medium bowl, beat peanut butter and cream cheese until light. Beat in eggs, granulated sugar, flour, milk and vanilla. Melt butter or margarine in a griddle or large skillet over medium heat. Spoon about 1/4 cup batter onto hot griddle or skillet. Cook on one side until bubbly; turn and cook other side until golden.

Place 1 pancake on each plate. Top one half of each pancake with several slices of peaches, bananas and kiwi fruit. Sprinkle with powdered sugar. Fold in half. Top with boysenberry or raspberry syrup. Makes 6 servings.

Cakes & Pies

Cakes are often associated with special occasions such as birthdays, holidays or weddings. These cakes are scrumptious looking and lend a special festive touch to celebrations.

In addition to important celebrations, I enjoy the simplicity of a basic peanut butter cake at a picnic, pot-luck supper or family dinner. It is an impressive dessert, without seeming too pretentious. And best of all, you can make it ahead of time, leaving you free to visit with guests and put the finishing touches on other dishes.

Cheesecakes take on new appeal when peanut butter is combined with chocolate. Pies, too, are timeless favorites with peanut butter as the featured flavor or paired with apples or peaches. They will wow your guests and make a special occasion even more memorable.

Muddy River Cake

It may look like a muddy river, but it tastes heavenly.

3/4 cup margarine or butter
4 (1-oz.) squares semisweet chocolate
4 eggs
1/2 cup peanut butter
1 1/2 cups sugar
1 teaspoon vanilla extract
1 1/2 cups all-purpose flour
Chocolate Frosting (see below)
1 (7-oz.) jar marshmallow creme
1/4 cup chopped peanuts (optional)
Chocolate Frosting

Chocolate Frosting
2 tablespoons margarine or butter, melted
2 (1-oz.) squares semisweet chocolate, melted
1/3 cup crunchy peanut butter
3 cups powdered sugar, sifted
5 tablespoons milk

Melt margarine or butter and chocolate together in a small saucepan over low heat, stirring frequently. Set aside to cool slightly.

Preheat oven to 350°F (175°C). Grease and flour a 13 x 9-inch baking pan. In a large bowl, beat eggs until thickened and lemon colored. Beat in peanut butter and sugar, then chocolate mixture and vanilla. Stir in flour until batter is smooth. Spread evenly in prepared pan. Bake about 30 minutes or until top springs back when lightly pressed with finger.

Prepare frosting while cake is baking. Remove cake from oven and immediately spread marshmallow creme over top of cake. Drop spoonfuls of chocolate frosting over all and swirl with a spatula. Sprinkle with peanuts, if desired. Makes about 12 servings.

Chocolate Frosting
Combine frosting ingredients in a medium bowl; stir or beat until blended.

Harvest Moon Apple Cake

This slightly spicy cake is dotted with peanut butter chips.

3 eggs
1/2 cup vegetable oil
2 cups sugar
2 cups all-purpose flour
1/2 teaspoon baking soda
1 teaspoon ground cinnamon
1/4 teaspoon freshly grated nutmeg
1 teaspoon vanilla extract
1 cup peanut butter chips (about 6 oz.)
2 small apples, peeled, cored and finely chopped

Topping

1/2 cup margarine or butter
1 cup lightly packed brown sugar
1/4 cup milk
2 cups powdered sugar, sifted

Preheat oven to 350°F (175°C). Grease a 13 x 9-inch baking pan.

In a large bowl, beat eggs until foamy; gradually beat in oil. Add sugar, flour, baking soda, cinnamon, nutmeg and vanilla. Mix until smooth. Stir in chips and apples. Spoon into prepared pan. Bake about 45 minutes or until top springs back when lightly pressed with finger. Cool in pan on a wire rack.

Prepare topping. Spread topping over cake. Cut into squares. Makes 20 to 24 servings.

Topping

In a medium saucepan over low heat, cook margarine or butter and brown sugar 2 minutes, stirring constantly. Add milk and bring to a simmer; remove from heat; stir in powdered sugar. Cool and beat until smooth and of spreading consistency.

Ground Peanut Cake with Creamy Filling

Rich with peanut flavor, this cake is made with peanuts and filled with a creamy peanut butter filling.

1 cup (5 1/4 oz.) peanuts
1/2 cup sugar
3 eggs, separated
2 tablespoons all-purpose flour
2 tablespoons butter, melted and cooled slightly
1/4 teaspoon cream of tartar
Grand Marnier Filling (see below)
Whipped cream to decorate
Whole peanuts to decorate

Creamy Filling

1/3 cup sugar
2 tablespoons cornstarch
3/4 cup milk
1/2 cup peanut butter
2 tablespoons Grand Marnier liqueur

Preheat oven to 350°F (175°C). Grease a 9-inch round cake pan; line bottom with parchment or waxed paper.

In a food processor, grind peanuts with 1/4 cup of the sugar until ground but not buttery. Add egg yolks and process until well mixed. Transfer mixture to a medium bowl. Stir in flour and melted butter; set aside.

In another bowl, beat egg whites and cream of tartar until soft peaks form. Beat in remaining 1/4 cup sugar, 1 tablespoon at a time, beating until stiff but not dry. Stir one-third of the beaten egg whites into nut mixture. Gently fold in remaining beaten whites. Spoon batter into prepared pan. Bake 20 to 22 minutes or until center springs back when gently pressed with finger. Invert cake onto a wire rack; cool.

Prepare filling. Slice cake horizontally through center. Spread filling on one cut side of cake. Top with other half, cut side down. Decorate with whipped cream and whole peanuts. Cut into wedges. Refrigerate leftovers. Makes 6 to 8 servings.

Creamy Filling

In a small saucepan, combine sugar and cornstarch. Stir in milk. Cook, stirring constantly, over medium heat until mixture simmers. Reduce heat and simmer, stirring constantly, 1 minute. Stir in peanut butter until melted. Remove from heat; cool. Stir in liqueur.

Favorite Peanut Butter Cake

Cover this cake with your favorite chocolate frosting for a special dessert.

1 cup peanut butter
1/2 cup margarine or butter, softened
2 cups lightly packed brown sugar
2 eggs
1 teaspoon vanilla extract
2 cups all-purpose flour
2 teaspoons baking powder
1/2 teaspoon baking soda
3/4 cup milk
Favorite frosting

Preheat oven to 350°F (175°C). Grease and flour 2 (9-inch) round cake pans.

Beat peanut butter, margarine or butter and brown sugar until light and fluffy. Add eggs and vanilla; beat until well mixed. Combine flour, baking powder and soda. Add dry ingredients alternately with milk, beating well after each addition. Pour batter into prepared pans. Bake about 30 minutes or until centers spring back when gently pressed with finger.

Cool layers in pans 5 minutes. Turn out onto wire racks and cool. Frost with favorite frosting. Makes 2 (9-inch) layers.

Chocolate Jelly Roll with Peanut Butter Filling

You can make this cake a day ahead; roll it in a clean dish towel and refrigerate it until you make the filling.

1/2 cup all-purpose flour
2 tablespoons unsweetened cocoa powder
4 egg whites, at room temperature
1/4 teaspoon cream of tartar
2/3 cup sugar
4 egg yolks
1 teaspoon freshly squeezed lemon juice
Powdered sugar for dusting towel

Peanut Butter Filling
1/2 cup sugar
2 tablespoons cornstarch
1 cup milk
1/3 cup peanut butter
1 teaspoon vanilla extract

Preheat oven to 350°F (175°C). Grease a 15 x 10-inch jelly roll pan. Line bottom with waxed paper; lightly grease paper.

Stir together flour and cocoa powder; set aside. In a large bowl, beat egg whites and cream of tartar until soft peaks form. Gradually beat in 1/3 cup of the granulated sugar until stiff, but not dry, peaks form. In a medium bowl, beat egg yolks until thick and lemon colored. Gradually beat in remaining 1/3 cup granulated sugar and lemon juice. Beat in flour mixture. Fold beaten yolk mixture into beaten egg whites. Spread evenly in prepared pan. Bake 15 minutes or until center springs back when lightly pressed with finger.

Place a clean towel on a flat surface; sprinkle with powdered sugar. Immediately turn baked cake onto sugared towel; remove waxed paper. Carefully roll up warm cake and towel from narrow end of cake. When cool, carefully unroll cake and remove towel.

Prepare filling. Spread filling over cake. Reroll; wrap in foil or plastic and refrigerate. Cut into rounds. Makes 8 servings.

Peanut Butter Filling

In a small saucepan, combine sugar and cornstarch. Stir in milk and cook, stirring constantly, over medium heat until thickened and bubbly. Remove from heat. Stir in peanut butter and vanilla until peanut butter melts. Cool, stirring occasionally, or place plastic wrap directly on top of filling while it cools.

Calypso Chocolate Chip Ring

The addition of bananas to this cake provides an exciting tropical flavor.

1/3 cup peanut butter
1/3 cup margarine or butter, softened
1/2 cup sugar
2 eggs
1/4 cup milk
1 banana, mashed
1 1/2 cups all-purpose flour
1 1/2 teaspoons baking powder
1/2 teaspoon baking soda
1/2 cup semisweet chocolate pieces
Powdered sugar (optional)

Preheat oven to 350°F (175°C). Grease a 6-cup tube pan or mold.

In a large bowl, beat peanut butter, margarine or butter and sugar until light. Beat in eggs, milk and banana until blended. Add flour, baking powder and soda; beat on low speed until combined. Stir in chocolate pieces. Spoon batter into prepared pan. Bake about 35 minutes or until center springs back when gently pressed with finger.

Cool cake in pan on a wire rack 5 minutes. Remove from pan; cool on rack. Sprinkle with powdered sugar, if desired. Makes 6 to 8 servings.

Popular Peanut Butter Frosting

With lots of peanut butter flavor, this creamy frosting is good on chocolate cakes.

1/3 cup peanut butter
1/4 cup margarine or butter, softened
1/2 teaspoon vanilla extract
1 (1-lb.) package powdered sugar, sifted
1/3 cup milk
Chopped peanuts (optional)

In a medium bowl, combine peanut butter, margarine or butter and vanilla. Beat until blended. Add sugar and milk and beat until of good spreading consistency. Spread on a cooled cake. Sprinkle with chopped peanuts, if desired. Makes enough frosting to cover a 2-layer, 8- or 9-inch cake.

Upside-Down Peach Peanut Butter Cake

Especially good when it's fresh from the oven and still slightly warm.

1 (15- to 16-oz.) can sliced canned peaches
1/2 cup lightly packed brown sugar
2 tablespoons margarine or butter, melted
1/4 cup solid vegetable shortening
1/4 cup peanut butter

2/3 cup granulated sugar
1 egg
2/3 cup milk
1 1/4 cups all-purpose flour
1 1/2 teaspoons baking powder

Preheat oven to 350°F (175°C). Grease a 9-inch round cake pan.

Pour peaches into a strainer; let stand until well drained. In a small bowl, combine brown sugar and margarine or butter. Spread on bottom of prepared pan; arrange drained peach slices on top.

In a large bowl, beat shortening, peanut butter and granulated sugar until light and fluffy. Beat in egg, milk, flour and baking powder until smooth. Carefully spoon batter over peaches. Bake about 40 minutes or until center springs back when lightly pressed with finger.

Cool cake in pan on a wire rack 5 minutes. Loosen edge of cake with a knife; invert onto a plate. Makes 6 to 8 servings.

Cocoa Peanut Butter Cheesecake

The smooth and rich peanut butter and chocolate filling is paired with a cinnamony crust.

1 1/2 cups vanilla wafer crumbs
1/4 cup margarine, melted
1/2 teaspoon ground cinnamon
1 (8-oz.) package cream cheese, softened
1/2 cup peanut butter
1/2 cup dairy sour cream
2 eggs
3/4 cup sugar
3 tablespoons cocoa powder
1 teaspoon vanilla extract

In a small bowl, combine wafer crumbs, margarine and cinnamon. Press over bottom and up sides of a 9-inch pie pan; refrigerate until chilled.

Preheat oven to 325°F (165°C). In a large bowl, beat cream cheese and peanut butter until blended. Add sour cream, eggs, sugar, cocoa powder and vanilla. Beat until smooth. Pour filling into chilled crust. Bake 45 to 50 minutes or until center is set. Cool and cut into wedges. Refrigerate leftovers. Makes 6 to 8 servings.

Peanut Butter Swirl Cheesecake

Classic cheesecake is updated with swirls of peanut butter.

1 1/2 cups chocolate cookie crumbs (about 26 [2 1/4-inch] wafers)
3 tablespoons margarine or butter, melted
2 oz. semisweet chocolate
1/3 cup crunchy peanut butter
2 (8-oz.) packages cream cheese, softened
3/4 cup sugar
2 eggs
1 cup dairy sour cream
1 teaspoon vanilla extract

In a small bowl, combine cookie crumbs and margarine or butter. Press over bottom and 1 1/2 inches up sides of an 8-inch springform pan; refrigerate until chilled.

Preheat oven to 350°F (175°C). Combine chocolate and peanut butter in a small saucepan. Melt over low heat, stirring frequently; set aside.

In a large bowl, beat cream cheese and sugar until combined. Add eggs; beat until smooth. Stir in sour cream and vanilla. Pour filling into chilled crust. Drop melted chocolate–peanut butter mixture into 6 or 7 mounds on top of filling. Swirl with a metal spatula or table knife.

Bake 50 to 60 minutes or until center is set. Cool and cut into wedges. Refrigerate leftovers. Makes 6 to 8 servings.

Pear Date No-Crust Pie

Dress up this home-style dessert with a topping of sour cream or vanilla ice cream.

1/2 cup rolled oats
1/4 cup all-purpose flour
1/3 cup lightly packed brown sugar
1/4 teaspoon freshly grated nutmeg
1/4 teaspoon ground allspice

3 tablespoons margarine or butter
1/3 cup peanut butter
1/2 cup chopped dates or raisins
3 large pears, peeled,
   cored and coarsely chopped

Preheat oven to 375°F (190°C). In a medium bowl, combine oats, flour, sugar, nutmeg and allspice. With a pastry blender, cut margarine or butter and peanut butter into mixture until it resembles coarse crumbs. Combine dates or raisins and pears in an 8-inch pie pan. Sprinkle oat mixture over top. Bake 30 to 35 minutes or until pears are tender. Serve warm. Makes 5 or 6 servings.

Nectarine Peanut Crumb Pie

Make this special treat when nectarines are ripe.

1 (9-inch) unbaked pie crust
1/2 cup sugar
1/3 cup all-purpose flour
1/4 teaspoon freshly grated nutmeg
6 cups sliced nectarines (about 6 large nectarines)

Topping

3 tablespoons margarine or butter
1/4 cup crunchy peanut butter
1/2 cup all-purpose flour
1/3 cup lightly packed brown sugar

Preheat oven to 425°F (220°C). Line a 9-inch pie pan with pie crust.

In a large bowl, mix together sugar, flour and nutmeg. Add nectarines; toss to mix. Spoon filling into unbaked pie shell. Prepare Topping and crumble over nectarine mixture. Bake 20 minutes. Cover pie with foil. Reduce temperature to 350°F (175°C); bake 30 minutes or until golden brown. Makes 6 to 8 servings.

Topping

In a small bowl, with a pastry blender, cut margarine or butter and peanut butter into flour and brown sugar until mixture resembles coarse crumbs.

Creamy Peanut Butter Pie

A special combination of crunchy peanut crust with an enticing smooth filling.

Chocolate Crust (see below)
16 large marshmallows or 1 1/2 cups miniature marshmallows
2/3 cup milk
3/4 cup peanut butter
3/4 cup whipping cream

Chocolate Crust

1/2 (11-oz.) package pie crust mix
1/4 cup lightly packed brown sugar
1 oz. semisweet chocolate, grated
1/2 cup finely chopped peanuts
1 teaspoon vanilla extract
1 tablespoon water

Prepare crust. In a saucepan, combine marshmallows, milk and peanut butter and cook over low heat, stirring, until marshmallows melt and mixture is smooth. Cool at room temperature 20 to 30 minutes, stirring occasionally, until mixture is almost room temperature.

In a medium bowl, whip cream until stiff. Quickly fold in peanut butter mixture. Pour filling into cooled crust; refrigerate several hours or until firm. Cut into wedges. Refrigerate leftovers. Makes 8 servings.

Chocolate Crust

Preheat oven to 375°F (190°C). Grease a 9-inch pie pan. In a medium bowl, with a fork, combine pie crust mix, brown sugar, chocolate, peanuts, vanilla and water. Press over bottom and up sides of prepared pie pan. Bake in preheated oven 15 minutes. Cool.

Apple Crumb Pie

A family favorite with a peanut butter topping.

1 (9-inch) unbaked pie crust
6 medium, green cooking apples, peeled, cored and thinly sliced
1/2 cup sugar
1/2 teaspoon ground cinnamon
1/4 teaspoon freshly grated nutmeg
Crumb Topping (see below)

Crumb Topping

2/3 cup lightly packed brown sugar
1/3 cup all-purpose flour
2 tablespoons margarine or butter
1/3 cup crunchy peanut butter

Preheat oven to 400°F (205°C). Line a 9-inch pie pan with pie crust, allowing a 1/2-inch overhang. Fold under extra pastry; crimp edges.

Combine apples with sugar, cinnamon and nutmeg. Spoon into prepared crust. Prepare topping and crumble over apples. Bake 10 to 15 minutes. Cover with foil. Bake 40 to 45 minutes or until apples are tender. Makes 6 to 8 servings.

Crumb Topping

In a small bowl, combine brown sugar and flour. With a pastry blender, cut in margarine or butter and peanut butter until mixture resembles coarse crumbs.

Frozen & Refrigerated Desserts

Everyone craves ice cream! And peanut butter ice cream is no exception. There's a variety, ranging from the traditional basic flavor to everyone's favorite, Fudgy Peanut Butter Ice Cream. All of our ice creams can be made in a regular ice cream freezer or in your refrigerator freezer. When using the refrigerator freezer to make ice cream, freeze ingredients in ice trays or a shallow bowl. Freeze until solid. Remove from freezer; break mixture into pieces. Beat in an electric mixer or food processor. Return to freezer tray; freeze again.

For a show-off dessert, start with one of our ice creams or one from the ice cream store or market, then spoon Butterscotch Peanutty Topping or Peanut Butter Fudge Topping over it for an especially rich flavor and texture.

Chocolate—Peanut Butter Cup Freeze

*To slightly soften ice cream, let it stand in the refrigerator 10 or 15 minutes
before pressing it over chilled cookie crust.*

1-1/2 cups thin chocolate cookies, crushed (about 26 [2-1/4-inch] wafers)
1/4 cup margarine or butter, melted
1/2 gal. vanilla ice cream, very slightly softened
3 oz. chocolate peanut butter cups, chopped (about 3/4 cup chopped)
Topping (see below)

Topping

1 cup thick fudge sauce or topping
1 to 2 tablespoons coffee-flavored liqueur

In a medium bowl, combine crushed cookies and margarine or butter. Press over bottom of a 9-inch springform pan. Thoroughly chill in freezer at least 1 hour.

Spoon half of ice cream over chilled crust. Top with chopped peanut butter cups, then remaining ice cream. Freeze at least 3 or 4 hours or overnight.

Make topping. Remove sides from pan. Cut into wedges. Spoon topping over each serving.
Makes 8 to 10 servings.

Topping

In a small serving bowl, combine fudge sauce and liqueur.

Waffle Sundaes

Make these waffles at your convenience, then package and freeze them until they are needed.

1/4 cup peanut butter
2 tablespoons brown sugar
2 tablespoons vegetable oil
1 egg, slightly beaten

1 cup milk
1 cup pancake or waffle mix
Ice cream
Chocolate or fudge sauce

In a medium bowl, combine peanut butter, sugar and oil. Whisk until blended. Whisk in egg and milk. Stir in pancake mix. Heat waffle iron according to manufacturer's directions and lightly grease. Spoon about 2/3 cup batter onto lightly greased hot waffle iron and cook until golden. Repeat with remaining batter. Cut each waffle into 4 sections. Top each section with a scoop of ice cream and chocolate or fudge sauce. Makes 12 servings.

Frozen Chocolate Peanut Butter Ribbons

Whip it up ahead of time and freeze until needed.

1/2 cup crunchy peanut butter
1/4 cup margarine or butter, softened
2/3 cup lightly packed brown sugar
2 eggs
1 teaspoon vanilla extract
2/3 cup all-purpose flour
1/2 teaspoon baking powder
1/4 teaspoon freshly grated nutmeg
1 tablespoon miniature multicolored candies or sprinkles
1 quart chocolate or vanilla ice cream, slightly softened
1/2 to 3/4 cup chocolate sauce

Preheat oven to 350°F (175°C). Line a 9-inch loaf pan with waxed paper.

In large mixing bowl, beat peanut butter, margarine or butter and sugar until combined. Add eggs and vanilla and beat until light and fluffy. Stir in flour, baking powder and nutmeg. Spoon mixture into prepared pan. Sprinkle with miniature multicolored candies. Bake 22 to 24 minutes or until cake pulls away from sides of pan.

Turn cake out onto a wire rack; cool. Cut cake horizontally into 2 equal layers. Carefully spread ice cream on cut side of bottom layer. Top with second layer, cut side down. Wrap in foil; freeze at least 2 to 3 hours. Cut into crosswise slices. Top with chocolate sauce. Makes 8 or 9 servings.

Peanut Butter Ice Cream

Very smooth and rich-tasting with good peanut butter flavor.

2 eggs, beaten
1 cup lightly packed brown sugar
2/3 cup peanut butter
1 (12-oz.) can evaporated milk
1 teaspoon vanilla extract
1 1/2 cups half and half or whipping cream

In a medium saucepan, combine eggs, brown sugar, peanut butter and evaporated milk. Cook, stirring, over low heat until smooth and thickened; cool slightly. Add vanilla and half and half or whipping cream.

Freeze mixture in ice cream maker according to manufacturer's directions. Or pour into plastic container or ice cube trays; cover and freeze solid in refrigerator freezer. Break into pieces; process on high speed in the bowl of an electric mixer or food processor fitted with metal blade until soft but not melted. Quickly return to freezer and freeze to desired consistency. Makes 5 to 5 1/2 cups.

Fudgy Peanut Butter Ice Cream

A blend of flavors that have been a favorite combo for generations.

1 cup sugar
1 tablespoon cornstarch
2 cups milk
2 eggs, beaten slightly
1 (6-oz.) package semisweet chocolate chips
1/2 cup peanut butter
1 cup whipping cream
1 teaspoon vanilla extract

In a medium saucepan, combine sugar, cornstarch, milk and eggs. Cook, stirring, over medium heat until mixture begins to simmer. Reduce heat to low. Whisk in chocolate chips and cook, stirring, 1 minute. Remove from heat. Whisk in peanut butter. Add whipping cream and vanilla. Cool to room temperature.

Freeze mixture in ice cream maker according to manufacturer's directions. Or pour into plastic container or ice cube trays, cover and freeze solid in refrigerator freezer. Break into pieces; process on high speed in the bowl of an electric mixer or food processor fitted with metal blade until soft but not melted. Quickly return to freezer and freeze to desired consistency. Makes 5 to 5 1/2 cups.

Banana Peanut Butter Ice Cream

Ripe bananas are easier to mash and have a more pronounced flavor.

1/2 cup crunchy peanut butter
2 bananas, sliced
3/4 cup sugar
1 teaspoon vanilla extract
3 cups half and half

In a large bowl, beat together peanut butter, bananas and sugar until smooth. Stir in vanilla and half and half.

Freeze mixture in ice cream maker according to manufacturer's directions. Or pour into plastic container or ice cube trays; cover and freeze solid in refrigerator freezer. Break into pieces; process on high speed in the bowl of an electric mixer or food processor fitted with metal blade until soft but not melted. Quickly return to freezer; freeze to desired consistency. Makes 5 to 5 1/2 cups.

Variation

For a richer and smoother ice cream, substitute 1 cup whipping cream for 1 cup of the half and half.

Rocky Road Peanut Butter Ice Cream

You'll love the contrasting texture and flavor of marshmallows and peanuts with chocolate.

1 cup sugar
1/3 cup unsweetened cocoa powder
2 cups milk
2 eggs, slightly beaten
1/2 cup peanut butter
1 cup whipping cream
1 (5-oz.) can evaporated milk
1 cup miniature marshmallows
1/2 cup coarsely chopped unsalted dry-roasted peanuts

In a large saucepan, mix sugar and cocoa. Stir in milk and eggs. Cook, stirring, over medium-low heat until cocoa dissolves and mixture is slightly thickened. Remove from heat. Whisk or beat in peanut butter. Add whipping cream and evaporated milk. Cool to room temperature.

Freeze mixture in ice cream maker according to manufacturer's directions. Quickly stir in miniature marshmallows and peanuts. Serve immediately or freeze in containers to desired consistency. Makes about 6 cups.

Pronto Brown Sugar Peanut Sauce

A favorite dessert topping—finish it with a sprinkle of chopped peanuts.

1/2 cup margarine or butter
2 cups lightly packed brown sugar
1 (5-oz.) can evaporated milk
3/4 cup crunchy peanut butter

In a 1-quart saucepan, combine all ingredients. Bring to boil over medium heat, stirring constantly. Reduce heat and simmer 2 minutes. Serve warm over ice cream or angel food cake. Refrigerate leftovers. Makes 2 2/3 cups.

Peanut Butter Fudge Topping

So easy to make; so wonderful to taste.

1/4 cup margarine or butter
1/3 cup crunchy peanut butter
1/3 cup lightly packed brown sugar
1/3 cup granulated sugar
1/3 cup unsweetened cocoa powder
1/2 cup milk

In a 2-quart saucepan, combine margarine or butter and peanut butter. Melt over low heat, stirring. Whisk in brown and granulated sugars, cocoa and milk. Cook, stirring, until sauce simmers. Serve over ice cream or cake. Refrigerate leftovers. Makes 1 1/2 cups.

Butterscotch Peanutty Topping

A welcome flourish to a dish of chocolate or vanilla ice cream.

1/4 cup lightly packed brown sugar
1/2 cup light corn syrup
2 tablespoons water
1/3 cup crunchy peanut butter
1/3 cup half and half
1 tablespoon margarine or butter
1/2 teaspoon vanilla extract

Combine brown sugar, corn syrup and water in a 2-quart saucepan over medium heat, stirring constantly, 3 or 4 minutes or until syrupy. Whisk in peanut butter, then half and half and margarine or butter; remove from heat. Stir in vanilla; cool. Pour mixture into a container with a lid, cover and refrigerate until needed. Stir before spooning over ice cream. Makes about 1 1/4 cups.

Tropical Rice Pudding

A wonderful updated version of old-fashioned rice pudding.

1/2 cup uncooked long-grain white rice
3 eggs, beaten slightly
2 cups milk
1/3 cup sugar
1/4 cup peanut butter
1/2 teaspoon vanilla extract
1 banana, diced
Toasted shredded coconut

Cook rice according to package directions; cool. In a medium saucepan, combine eggs, milk and sugar. Cook over medium heat, stirring, about 15 minutes or until mixture coats a metal spoon; remove from heat. Whisk in peanut butter and vanilla. Stir in cooked rice and banana. Spoon into a bowl; refrigerate until cool. Spoon pudding into dessert dishes; sprinkle with coconut. Makes 5 or 6 servings.

Irish Cream Bread Pudding

An easy-to-make, yet very impressive dessert.

1/3 cup peanut butter
3 tablespoons sugar
1/4 cup Irish Cream liqueur
3 eggs
1 1/2 cups milk or half and half
1/2 teaspoon vanilla extract
3 slices bread, cut into 1/2-inch cubes
1/4 cup flaked coconut

Preheat oven to 325°F (165°C). Grease an 8-inch round cake pan.

In a medium bowl, beat peanut butter and sugar until smooth. Beat in liqueur, eggs, milk and vanilla. Sprinkle bread cubes over bottom of prepared pan. Spoon peanut butter mixture over bread. Sprinkle with coconut. Bake about 40 minutes or until set in center. Refrigerate 2 to 3 hours or until cool. Makes 5 or 6 servings.

Cookies

Many people only bake cookies for special occasions such as Christmas. I think that cookies are appropriate for any day of the year and almost any situation. That's why I like to keep some in the cookie jar, ready to serve at a moment's notice.

Peanut butter cookies rank high in popularity. Everyone enjoys the well-known favorite with the crisscross design on top. I have included that one plus a variety of bars and thumbprints, where peanut butter is paired with the ever-popular jelly as well as with chocolate.

For best results in baking cookies, be sure to follow the directions in these recipes. When making individual drop cookies, try to make all the same size for the most even browning. If you reuse the same baking sheets for a whole batch of cookies, be sure to let the sheets cool completely so the dough doesn't spread too much. Bar cookies are easier to cut when they are completely cooled.

Traditional Peanut Butter Cookies

The all-time favorite for lunch boxes, picnics and snacking.

1/2 cup granulated sugar
1/2 cup lightly packed brown sugar
1/2 cup margarine or butter, softened
1/2 cup peanut butter

1 egg
1/2 teaspoon baking soda
1 1/2 cups all-purpose flour
1/2 teaspoon vanilla extract

Preheat oven to 375°F (190°C). Combine sugars, margarine or butter, peanut butter and egg in a large bowl and beat until light. Add remaining ingredients and beat until combined.

Shape dough into 1-inch balls. Place about 2 inches apart on ungreased baking sheets. Lightly press dough with fork tines, creating a crisscross pattern. Bake 9 to 11 minutes or until golden brown. Remove from baking sheets and cool on a wire rack. Makes 42 to 44 cookies.

Easy Peanut Butter & Jelly Thumbprints

An easy variation of the ever-popular thumbprint cookies.

1/2 cup peanut butter
1/3 cup margarine or butter, softened
1/4 cup lightly packed brown sugar

1/2 teaspoon vanilla extract
1 1/4 cups all-purpose flour
1/3 cup grape or strawberry jelly

Preheat oven to 350°F (175°C). Combine peanut butter, margarine or butter, brown sugar and vanilla in a large bowl and beat together until light and fluffy. Stir in flour.

Spread dough in an ungreased 8-inch square pan, pressing evenly with fingertips. Press thumbprints over surface of dough until they almost touch. Fill each indentation with jelly. Bake 22 to 24 minutes or until browned. Remove from pan and cool on a wire rack. Cut into bars. Makes 25 to 36 cookies.

Chocolate Peanut Butter Pinwheels

If the dough becomes soft during slicing, return it to the refrigerator or freezer until firm.

1/2 cup margarine or butter, softened
3/4 cup lightly packed brown sugar
1 egg
1 teaspoon vanilla extract
1 1/2 cups all-purpose flour
2 tablespoons unsweetened cocoa powder
2 tablespoons peanut butter

Combine margarine or butter, brown sugar, egg and vanilla in a medium bowl and beat until light and fluffy. Add flour and mix until blended. Divide dough in half. Mix cocoa powder into one half. Mix peanut butter into other half. Cover and refrigerate both halves until firm.

On floured waxed paper, roll out each half of dough into a 16 x 6-inch rectangle. With waxed-paper side up, place peanut butter rectangle on chocolate dough; peel waxed paper off peanut dough. Tightly roll up doughs together, peeling waxed paper off chocolate dough as you roll. Cover and freeze or refrigerate several hours.

Preheat oven to 400°F (205°C). Cut dough crosswise into 1/4-inch slices. Bake 7 to 8 minutes or until lightly browned. Remove from baking sheets and cool on a wire rack. Makes 60 to 64 cookies.

Peanut Butter Meringue Drops

These cookielike mini-meringues are crispy on the outside and chewy on the inside.

3 egg whites, at room temperature
1/4 teaspoon cream of tartar
1 teaspoon vanilla extract
1/2 cup plus 3 tablespoons sugar
3 tablespoons crunchy peanut butter

Preheat oven to 300°F (150°C). Line a 17 x 14-inch baking sheet with parchment paper.

In a large bowl, combine egg whites with cream of tartar and vanilla. Beat until soft peaks form. Gradually beat in 1/2 cup sugar, 1 tablespoon at a time, beating on high speed until very stiff peaks form.

In a small bowl, beat peanut butter and 3 tablespoons sugar until well blended. Stir one-third of beaten egg whites into peanut butter. Fold peanut butter into remaining egg whites. Drop mixture by tablespoonfuls on prepared baking sheet. Bake 35 to 40 minutes or until set.

Turn off oven; leave baked meringues in closed oven 50 minutes. Remove from paper. Store leftovers in an airtight container. Makes 28 (2-inch) meringues.

Treasure Islands

Eye-catching, easy-to-make cookies that are loaded with tasty prize ingredients.

1/2 cup margarine or butter, softened
1/3 cup crunchy peanut butter
3/4 cup lightly packed brown sugar
1 egg
1/3 cup dairy sour cream
1/2 teaspoon vanilla extract
1 3/4 cups all-purpose flour
1/2 teaspoon baking soda
1 cup chopped dates
1/2 cup flaked coconut
Orange Glaze (see below)

Orange Glaze

1 cup powdered sugar
1 to 1 1/2 tablespoons milk
2 teaspoons melted margarine or butter
1/4 teaspoon grated orange peel

Preheat oven to 350°F (175°C). In a large mixing bowl, cream margarine or butter, peanut butter and brown sugar. Beat in egg, sour cream and vanilla. Stir in flour and baking soda. Add dates and coconut. Drop dough by teaspoonfuls on ungreased baking sheets. Bake in preheated oven about 10 minutes or until lightly browned. Cool over a wire rack.

    While cookies are cooling, make glaze. Drizzle cookies with glaze. Makes 55 to 60 cookies.

Orange Glaze:

In a small bowl, mix powdered sugar with milk, melted margarine or butter and orange peel. Use immediately.

Apple Peanut Butter Oatmeal Drops

Handy treats for lunch boxes or after school.

1/3 cup crunchy peanut butter
2 eggs
1/2 cup vegetable oil
1/2 cup molasses
1 cup all-purpose flour
1 teaspoon baking powder
1/2 teaspoon baking soda
1/2 teaspoon ground cinnamon
3/4 cup quick-cooking rolled oats
1 cooking apple, peeled, cored and finely chopped
Thin Icing (see below)

Thin Icing

1 cup powdered sugar, sifted
2 tablespoons milk

Preheat oven to 375°F (190°C). In a large bowl, combine peanut butter, eggs, oil and molasses. Beat until well blended. Stir in flour, baking powder, baking soda, cinnamon and oats. Add apple. Drop rounded teaspoonfuls of dough about 2 inches apart on ungreased baking sheets. Bake 10 to 12 minutes or until golden.

Remove cookies from baking sheets and cool on wire racks. Prepare icing and drizzle over cooled cookies. Makes about 45 cookies.

Thin Icing

In a small bowl, combine powdered sugar and milk.

Peanut Butter & Jelly Thumbprints

A favorite cookie with peanut butter fans.

3/4 cup granulated sugar
1/4 cup packed brown sugar
1 cup peanut butter

1 egg, beaten slightly
1/2 teaspoon vanilla extract
1/3 cup raspberry or grape jelly

Preheat oven to 350°F (175°C). In a medium bowl, combine all ingredients except jelly and stir until no longer sticky. Shape mixture into 1-inch balls. Place balls on ungreased baking sheets about 2 inches apart. Press thumb deeply into center of each ball. Bake 10 to 12 minutes. Remove to racks; fill each thumbprint with jelly. Makes about 36.

Pronto Super Chocolate Chip Cookies

Keep unbaked cookies in the freezer to bake fresh and serve for unexpected guests.
Unbaked cookies can be frozen up to one month.

3/4 cup margarine or butter, softened
1/2 cup peanut butter
1 1/4 cups lightly packed brown sugar
2 eggs
1 teaspoon vanilla extract

2 cups all-purpose flour
1 teaspoon baking soda
1 (12-oz.) package semisweet chocolate pieces
1/2 cup coarsely chopped peanuts

In a large bowl, combine margarine or butter, peanut butter, brown sugar, eggs, vanilla, flour and baking soda and beat until combined. Stir in chocolate pieces and peanuts. Using a small ice cream scoop or large kitchen spoon, make 1 1/2-inch balls. Place on waxed paper–lined baking sheets and freeze 1 to 2 hours or until firm. Place balls in a freezer bag; return to freezer.

Preheat oven to 325°F (165°C). Place frozen cookie balls about 3 inches apart on ungreased baking sheets. Bake 18 to 20 minutes if frozen or 15 to 17 minutes if thawed. Remove from baking sheets; cool on wire racks. Makes about 38 thick cookies.

Shortbread Peanut Butter Balls

If there are any long strips of orange peel in the marmalade, cut them into small pieces before combining with other ingredients.

1/2 cup crunchy peanut butter
1/4 cup light corn syrup
1/4 cup orange marmalade
1/2 cup shortbread cookie crumbs (about 8 cookies)
1 cup nonfat dry milk powder
1/3 cup finely chopped peanuts

In a medium bowl, combine peanut butter, corn syrup, marmalade, crushed cookies and nonfat dry milk. Shape into 1-inch balls. Roll in chopped peanuts. Refrigerate until firm. Makes about 30 balls.

Waikiki Shortbread Wedges

To toast coconut, spread on a baking sheet and bake in a 325°F (165°C) oven 12 to 14 minutes, stirring several times.

1/3 cup crunchy peanut butter
1/3 cup margarine or butter, softened
1/3 cup sugar
1 cup all-purpose flour
1 1/2 teaspoons grated gingerroot
1 teaspoon vanilla extract
1 cup flaked coconut, toasted
Powdered sugar

Preheat oven to 325°F (165°C). In a large bowl, beat peanut butter, margarine or butter and sugar until light. Beat in flour, gingerroot, vanilla and coconut. Pat mixture over bottom of an ungreased 9-inch springform or round cake pan. Bake 25 to 30 minutes or until golden brown.

Cool shortbread in pan on a wire rack about 10 minutes. Cut into 12 to 14 wedges in pan and cool completely. Sift powdered sugar over cookies. Remove from pan. Makes 12 to 14 cookies.

Peanut Butter Cookie Pizza

Create a party atmosphere with a sprinkling of colorful baking bits and pieces.

1/2 cup peanut butter
1/2 cup solid vegetable shortening
1 cup lightly packed brown sugar
1 egg
1/4 cup milk
1 teaspoon vanilla extract
1 2/3 cups all-purpose flour
1/2 teaspoon baking soda
Assorted small candies and chopped peanuts
Topping (see below)

Topping

2 cups powdered sugar, sifted
1/3 cup margarine or butter, softened
1/3 cup unsweetened cocoa powder
1/2 teaspoon vanilla extract
3 tablespoons milk

Preheat oven to 350°F (175°C). Grease a 12-inch pizza pan and line with parchment paper.

In a large bowl, beat together peanut butter, shortening and brown sugar until light. Beat in egg, milk and vanilla. Stir in flour and baking soda. Carefully spread dough over bottom and side of prepared pan, smoothing out with a rubber spatula or the back of a spoon. Bake in preheated oven 15 to 18 minutes.

Cool pizza in pan on a wire rack. While pizza is cooling, make topping. Spread topping over cooled cookie pizza. Sprinkle with candies and peanuts. Cut into small wedges. Makes 16 to 20 wedges.

Topping

In a medium bowl, combine powdered sugar, margarine or butter, cocoa powder, vanilla and milk. Beat until smooth.

Double Peanut Bars

A combination of favorite flavors will make you proud to serve these tempting bars.

2 cups all-purpose flour
2 cups lightly packed brown sugar
1/3 cup peanut butter
1/3 cup margarine or butter, softened
1 teaspoon baking powder
1 egg, beaten slightly
1 cup milk
1 teaspoon vanilla extract
1/2 cup chopped peanuts
3/4 cup milk chocolate or semisweet chocolate pieces
1/2 cup miniature marshmallows, halved

Preheat oven to 350°F (175°C). Grease a 13 x 9-inch baking pan; set aside.

In a large bowl, combine flour and brown sugar. With a pastry blender or two knives, cut in peanut butter and margarine or butter until mixture resembles coarse crumbs. Set aside 1 cup of crumbs in a small bowl. Add baking powder, egg, milk and vanilla to large bowl of crumbs; stir until mixed. Pour mixture into prepared pan. Add peanuts, chocolate pieces and marshmallows to crumbs in small bowl. Sprinkle over batter in pan. Bake 30 to 35 minutes or until firm. Cool in pan on a wire rack. Cut into bars or squares. Makes about 30 bars.

Raspberry Sour Cream Bars

Old-fashioned peanut bars with exciting raspberry cream topping.

1 1/2 cups all-purpose flour
1/4 cup powdered sugar
1/3 cup peanut butter
1/4 cup margarine or butter, softened
2/3 cup raspberry or strawberry jam or preserves
1 (3-oz.) package cream cheese, softened
2 tablespoons brown sugar
1 egg
2/3 cup dairy sour cream
1/2 teaspoon vanilla extract
1/4 cup coarsely chopped peanuts

Preheat oven to 350°F (175°C). In a medium bowl, combine flour and powdered sugar. With a pastry blender or two forks, cut in peanut butter and margarine or butter until mixture resembles coarse crumbs. Press over bottom of an ungreased 9-inch-square baking pan. Bake 18 to 20 minutes or until edges begin to brown.

Remove pan from oven; immediately drop small amounts of jam or preserves across top. In a small bowl, beat cream cheese, brown sugar and egg until light. Stir in sour cream and vanilla. Spoon over jam. Sprinkle with peanuts. Return to oven and bake 17 to 18 minutes or until topping is firm. Cool in pan on a wire rack. Cut into bars. Makes 24 to 32 bars.

Peanut Butter Oat Squares

A change-of-pace blend of flavors that have been favorites for generations.

1/2 cup margarine or butter, softened
1 cup lightly packed brown sugar
1/2 cup light corn syrup
1/4 cup crunchy peanut butter
1 teaspoon vanilla extract
3 cups quick-cooking rolled oats
1 (12-oz.) package semisweet chocolate pieces
1/3 cup crunchy peanut butter
1/2 cup chopped peanuts

Preheat oven to 375°F (190°C). In a large bowl, combine margarine or butter, brown sugar, corn syrup, 1/4 cup peanut butter and vanilla. Stir in oats. Press over bottom of an ungreased 9-inch-square baking pan. Bake 20 minutes.

While squares are baking, heat chocolate pieces with 1/3 cup peanut butter. Spread chocolate topping over hot bars; sprinkle with peanuts. Cool in pan; cut into squares. Makes 16 large or 25 small squares.

Blond Brownies

Just a touch of chocolate drizzled over the top adds a contrast of flavor and design.

1/3 cup margarine or butter
1 cup lightly packed brown sugar
1/3 cup crunchy peanut butter
2 eggs, slightly beaten
1 teaspoon vanilla extract
1/2 cup all-purpose flour
1/2 teaspoon baking powder
1/4 cup chopped peanuts
1/2 cup chocolate chips, melted

Preheat oven to 350°F (175°C). Grease an 8-inch-square pan.

In a medium saucepan, melt margarine or butter with brown sugar, stirring frequently. Remove from heat. Beat in peanut butter, eggs, vanilla, flour and baking powder. Spoon into prepared pan. Sprinkle with peanuts. Bake about 25 minutes or until edges are browned.

Cool in pan on a wire rack; drizzle with melted chocolate. Cut into bars or squares. Makes 20 to 25 bars.

Crispy Chocolate Bars

Crunchy peanut butter adds extra crunch to these crispy treats.

1 (6-oz.) package semisweet chocolate pieces
1/3 cup crunchy peanut butter
1/2 cup miniature marshmallows
1/2 teaspoon vanilla extract
2 cups Rice Krispies cereal

Grease an 8-inch-square pan; set aside. In a medium saucepan, combine chocolate pieces and peanut butter. Heat, stirring, over low heat until chocolate melts; remove from heat. Stir in marshmallows, vanilla and cereal. Press mixture into prepared pan. Refrigerate until firm. Cut into bars. Makes 18 to 24 bars.

Peanut Butter & Jelly Double Deckers

Your guests will be pleased to find jelly in the middle of these sandwich cookies.

1/2 cup peanut butter
1/3 cup margarine or butter, softened
1/2 cup sugar
1 egg
1/2 teaspoon vanilla extract
1 1/2 cups all-purpose flour
1/2 teaspoon baking soda
1/2 cup currant or grape jelly

In a large bowl, combine peanut butter, margarine or butter, sugar, egg, vanilla, flour and baking soda and beat until smooth. Form mixture into 2 rolls about 5 inches long and 1 3/4 inches across. Wrap in plastic wrap or foil; refrigerate at least 2 hours or until firm.

Preheat oven to 375°F (190°C). Remove rolls from refrigerator and unwrap. Cut each roll crosswise into 1/4-inch-thick slices. Place on ungreased baking sheets. Bake 12 to 14 minutes or until golden.

Remove from baking sheets; cool on wire racks. Spread bottoms of half of cookies with jelly. Top with remaining cookies, bottom side down. Makes about 20 cookies.

Crunchy Tropical Bars

To pack mixture evenly in a pan, lightly press top of mixture with the back of a large spoon.

1/3 cup margarine or butter
2/3 cup crunchy peanut butter
1/2 cup lightly packed brown sugar
1/2 cup chopped dates
1/2 teaspoon ground ginger
1/2 cup flaked coconut
2 1/2 cups Kix or Rice Krispies cereal

Line an 8-inch-square baking pan with foil. In a 2-quart saucepan, combine margarine or butter, peanut butter, sugar, dates and ginger. Heat, stirring, over low heat until combined; remove from heat. Stir in coconut and cereal. Pack into prepared pan, cover and refrigerate several hours or until firm. Remove from pan and peel off foil. Cut into bars. Makes about 35 to 40 bars.

Carnival Bars

Colorful candies add crunch and appetite appeal for a festive touch.

1/2 cup peanut butter
1/3 cup butter-flavored vegetable shortening
1/2 cup lightly packed brown sugar
1 egg
1 teaspoon vanilla extract
1/2 teaspoon baking powder
1 1/4 cups all-purpose flour
1/2 cup plain M&Ms candies, chopped

Preheat oven to 350°F (175°C). In a medium bowl, combine peanut butter, shortening, brown sugar, egg, vanilla, baking powder and flour. Beat until combined. Stir in M&Ms. Press mixture into an ungreased 9-inch-square pan. Bake 20 to 25 minutes or until golden brown. Cool in pan on a wire rack. Cut into bars or squares. Makes 24 to 32 cookies.

Peanut Butter Brownies

This updated peanut butter version of the traditional brownie results in many requests for seconds.

2 (1-oz.) squares unsweetened chocolate
1/4 cup margarine or butter, softened
1/3 cup peanut butter
1 cup lightly packed brown sugar
2 eggs
1 teaspoon vanilla extract
1/2 cup all-purpose flour

Preheat oven to 350°F (175°C). Grease an 8-inch-square pan.

In a small saucepan over low heat, melt chocolate; cool. In a medium bowl, combine margarine or butter, peanut butter and brown sugar and beat until light. Beat in eggs and vanilla. Beat in flour and melted chocolate until combined. Pour into prepared pan. Bake 30 to 35 minutes or until firm around the edges. Cool in pan on a wire rack. Cut into bars. Makes 25 to 35 bars.

Rocky Road Peanut Bars

You'll be proud to serve this quick and easy treat.

1 (12-oz.) package semisweet chocolate pieces
1 (14-oz.) can sweetened condensed milk
1/2 cup crunchy peanut butter
1 teaspoon vanilla extract
1 1/2 cups miniature marshmallows
1/4 cup coarsely chopped peanuts

Lightly grease a 9-inch-square pan. In a 2-quart saucepan, combine chocolate pieces and condensed milk. Heat, stirring constantly, over low heat until chocolate is melted. Quickly stir in peanut butter, vanilla, marshmallows and peanuts. Pour mixture into prepared pan. Cover and refrigerate 2 or 3 hours or until firm. Cut into bars. Makes 45 to 50 bars.

Candy

There's no mystique involved in making a batch of mouth-watering candy. Your success in candy making starts with a good recipe. Then it's up to you to carefully follow the directions for cooking as well as cooling the finished mixture.

For best results, use a heavy saucepan. Choose a pan that is large enough for the mixture to cook without boiling over. Then use a reliable candy thermometer that indicates the temperature accurately. Be sure to watch the temperature very carefully because it can increase quite rapidly. The difference of a few degrees can make quite a difference in the texture of the candy.

If possible, try to avoid a very humid day when making candy. When the humidity is high, the candy will absorb more moisture, resulting in an extra-soft product.

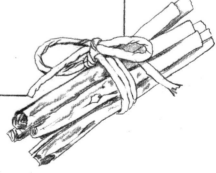

Marbled Peanut Butter Fudge

Our favorite—rich, creamy and delightfully peanutty.

4 cups sugar
1/2 cup unsweetened cocoa powder
1 1/3 cups milk
1/4 cup margarine or butter
2 teaspoons vanilla extract
1/2 cup peanut butter

Butter a 9-inch-square pan; set aside. In a 3-quart saucepan, combine sugar and cocoa. Add milk and stir until blended. Cook over medium heat, stirring occasionally, until sugar just dissolves. Add margarine or butter, reduce heat to medium-low and cook without stirring until mixture reaches the soft-ball stage or 238°F (114°C) on a candy thermometer. Remove from heat. Cool at room temperature without stirring until bottom of pan is warm, about 120°F (48°C).

Add vanilla and beat until candy just begins to lose its gloss around the edges. Pour into prepared pan. Quickly, drop tablespoons of peanut butter at regular intervals on top of fudge. Carefully cut through the fudge with a narrow spatula to create a marbled effect. Cool until firm. Cut into squares. Makes 36 pieces.

Shortcut Velvety Fudge

This is an easy and foolproof recipe for fudge that doesn't require a candy thermometer.

1 (5-oz.) can evaporated milk
1 1/2 cups sugar
2 tablespoons margarine or butter
1 1/2 cups semisweet chocolate chips
2/3 cup peanut butter
1 (7-oz.) jar marshmallow creme
1 teaspoon vanilla extract

Butter a 9-inch-square pan. In a medium saucepan combine milk, sugar and margarine or butter and bring to a boil over medium heat, stirring constantly. Boil 4 minutes, stirring occasionally; remove from heat. Add chocolate chips, stirring until almost melted. Stir in remaining ingredients. Spread mixture in prepared pan. Cool and cut into squares. Makes 49 to 64 squares.

Penuche, Peanut Butter Style

For generations, penuche has been a favorite candy.

2 cups lightly packed brown sugar
2 cups granulated sugar
1 cup milk
1 tablespoon light corn syrup
1 teaspoon vanilla extract
1/2 cup peanut butter

Butter an 8-inch-square pan. Combine brown and granulated sugars, milk and corn syrup in a 3-quart saucepan and bring to a boil, stirring constantly, over medium heat. Attach candy thermometer to pan. Cook over medium-low heat until mixture reaches soft-ball stage or 236°F (114°C) on candy thermometer; set aside. Cool to 115°F (45°C) or lukewarm. Add vanilla and peanut butter. Beat until smooth and candy thickens. Quickly pour mixture into prepared pan. Cool until firm. Cut into squares. Makes 35 to 45 pieces.

Peanut Butter Brittle

An excellent surprise gift for anyone who loves candy.

1/2 cup light corn syrup
1 cup sugar
1/2 cup water
1/2 cup crunchy peanut butter

1/4 cup coarsely chopped peanuts
1 tablespoon butter
1/4 teaspoon baking soda

Butter a 15 x 10-inch jelly-roll pan. Combine corn syrup, sugar and water in a 2-quart heavy saucepan and bring to boil over medium heat, stirring occasionally. Cover and cook 2 minutes. Uncover, insert candy thermometer and cook to 236°F (114°C) on thermometer.

Stir in peanut butter and peanuts and cook to 300°F (150°C); remove from heat. Stir in butter and baking soda. Immediately pour mixture into prepared jelly-roll pan; spread with a spatula. Cool. Break into clusters. Store in an airtight container. Makes 35 to 45 pieces.

Creamy Peanut Butter Pralines

Studded with peanuts, these pralines are a favorite variation of the traditional variety.

1 cup granulated sugar
1 cup lightly packed brown sugar
1/2 cup half and half

1/2 cup peanut butter
1/2 cup peanuts

Line a large baking sheet or tray with waxed paper; set aside. Combine granulated sugar, brown sugar and half and half in a large saucepan and bring to boil over medium heat, stirring constantly. Stir in peanut butter. Reduce heat and simmer until temperature reaches 236°F (114°C) on candy thermometer or to soft-ball stage.

Cool mixture 10 minutes. Beat with an electric mixer on low speed about 30 seconds or until slightly thickened but still glossy. Stir in peanuts. Drop mixture by tablespoonfuls on waxed paper. Makes about 25 pralines.

Home-Style Peanut Butter Cups

Imitate the ever-popular commercial candies and impress your friends with this recipe.

1/2 cup powdered sugar
1/3 cup dairy sour cream
1/4 teaspoon vanilla extract
3/4 cup crunchy peanut butter
1/2 lb. sweet baking chocolate or milk chocolate

In a small bowl, combine sugar, sour cream, vanilla and peanut butter. Refrigerate while preparing chocolate.

Melt chocolate in a pan or bowl over simmering water. With a narrow 1/2-inch brush, brush melted chocolate over bottom and 3/4 inch up sides of 2 1/4 x 1-inch paper cupcake liners. Place cups on a tray and refrigerate about 15 minutes or until firm.

Shape about 2 tablespoonfuls cool peanut butter mixture into a flattened ball. Fill each firm chocolate-lined cup. Spoon about 1 1/2 teaspoons remaining melted chocolate over top; refrigerate until firm. Makes 8 (2 1/4-inch) cups.

Irish Cream Truffles

A classic candy with surprise flavor and extra-smooth texture that you'll be proud to serve.

1 (12-oz.) package semisweet chocolate pieces
1/2 cup half and half
1/4 cup butter
1/4 cup crunchy peanut butter
2 tablespoons Irish Cream liqueur
Powdered sugar

Combine chocolate, half and half, butter and peanut butter in a 2-quart saucepan, and cook, stirring, over medium heat until smooth. Remove from heat. Stir in Irish cream, cover and refrigerate about 2 hours or until cold.

Form mixture into 1 1/4-inch balls. Roll in powdered sugar. Refrigerate until firm. Cover and refrigerate or freeze any leftovers. Makes 24 to 26 truffles.

Chocolate Peanut Butter Truffles

Interesting peanut-coated balls with deliciously creamy chocolate centers.

1 (12-oz.) package milk chocolate pieces
1/2 cup half and half
2 tablespoons butter
3/4 cup crunchy peanut butter
1 teaspoon vanilla extract
2/3 cup finely chopped peanuts

Combine milk chocolate pieces, half and half, butter and peanut butter in a medium saucepan and heat, stirring, over low heat until chocolate is melted. Add vanilla, cover and refrigerate about 2 hours or until cold.

Form mixture into 1-inch balls. Roll in peanuts. Refrigerate until firm. Cover and refrigerate or freeze any leftovers. Makes 28 to 30 truffles.

White Chocolate Cereal Squares

This combination of just three ingredients results in one of our most popular snacks.

4 oz. white chocolate, melted
1/2 cup crunchy peanut butter
3 cups Kix cereal or Cheerios cereal

Line an 8-inch-square pan with foil. In a large bowl, combine white chocolate and peanut butter. Stir in cereal. Press firmly into foil-lined pan. Refrigerate 2 or 3 hours. Cut into squares. Refrigerate leftovers. Makes about 25 to 30.

Maple Peanut Popcorn Clusters

This chewy confection is very popular with teenagers.

8 cups popped popcorn
1/3 cup light corn syrup
1/4 cup margarine or butter
1/4 cup maple syrup
1/3 cup crunchy peanut butter

Preheat oven to 250°F (120°C). While making the sauce, warm popcorn in a heatproof bowl in oven. Combine corn syrup, margarine or butter and maple syrup in a medium saucepan and heat over medium heat until margarine melts. Add peanut butter and heat, stirring, until bubbly. Pour mixture over warm popcorn. Immediately stir to coat evenly. Transfer coated popcorn to a baking sheet; bake 30 minutes, stirring once. Cool to room temperature. Store leftovers in an airtight container. Makes 6 to 8 servings.

Apricot Peanut Balls

Do not substitute another form of milk; the recipe is designed for sweetened condensed milk.

1 cup crunchy peanut butter
1 (14-oz.) can sweetened condensed milk
1/2 cup finely chopped dried apricots
1/4 cup sugar
1/4 teaspoon ground cinnamon

Combine peanut butter and condensed milk in a 2-quart pan and cook, stirring, over low heat until mixture is blended. Stir in apricots; remove from heat. Refrigerate mixture about 1 hour.

Shape mixture into 1-inch balls. In a shallow bowl, combine sugar and cinnamon. Roll each ball in sugar mixture. Refrigerate leftovers. Makes about 40 balls.

Metric Conversion Charts

Comparison to Metric Measure				
When You Know	Symbol	Multiply By	To Find	Symbol
teaspoons	tsp	5.0	milliliters	ml
tablespoons	tbsp	15.0	milliliters	ml
fluid ounces	fl. oz.	30.0	milliliters	ml
cups	c	0.24	liters	l
pints	pt.	0.47	liters	l
quarts	qt.	0.95	liters	l
ounces	oz.	28.0	grams	g
pounds	lb.	0.45	kilograms	kg
Fahrenheit	F	5/9 (after subtracting 32)	Celsius	C

Liquid Measure to Milliliters		
1/4 teaspoon	=	1.25 milliliters
1/2 teaspoon	=	2.5 milliliters
3/4 teaspoon	=	3.75 milliliters
1 teaspoon	=	5.0 milliliters
1-1/4 teaspoons	=	6.25 milliliters
1-1/2 teaspoons	=	7.5 milliliters
1-3/4 teaspoons	=	8.75 milliliters
2 teaspoons	=	10.0 milliliters
1 tablespoon	=	15.0 milliliters
2 tablespoons	=	30.0 milliliters

Fahrenheit to Celsius	
F	C
200-205	95
220-225	105
245-250	120
275	135
300-305	150
325-330	165
345-350	175
370-375	190
400-405	205
425-430	220
445-450	230
470-475	245
500	260

Liquid Measure to Milliliters		
1/4 cup	=	0.06 liters
1/2 cup	=	0.12 liters
3/4 cup	=	0.18 liters
1 cup	=	0.24 liters
1-1/4 cups	=	0.3 liters
1-1/2 cups	=	0.36 liters
2 cups	=	0.48 liters
2-1/2 cups	=	0.6 liters
3 cups	=	0.72 liters
3-1/2 cups	=	0.84 liters
4 cups	=	0.96 liters
4-1/2 cups	=	1.08 liters
5 cups	=	1.2 liters
5-1/2 cups	=	1.32 liters

Index

About the Author

Mable Hoffman is a professional home economist and director of Hoffman Food Consultants. She concentrates her efforts on food consulting, recipe development, and writing. She was a food stylist for many years.

Mable's cookbooks include *Appetizers; California Cooking; Chocolate Cookery; Crepe Cookery; Deep-Fry Cookery; Ice Cream; Pasta in Minutes; Cookies in Minutes; Frozen Yogurt; Carefree Entertaining; Crockery Cookery* and *Tomatoes*. Her cookbooks have won four Tastemaker Awards. Both *Crockery Cookery* and *Crepe Cookery* became #1 *New York Times* bestsellers. *Crockery Cookery* was revised in 1995.

Because Mable Hoffman loves the flavor of peanut butter in everything from soup to dessert, she especially enjoyed testing (and tasting) her creations for this book.